Quiet Desperation

The Effects of Competition in School on Abused and Neglected Children

Gerald W. Neal

Hamilton Books
A member of
The Rowman & Littlefield Publishing Group
Lanham • Boulder • New York • Toronto • Plymouth, UK

4501 Forbes Boulevard
Suite 200
Lanham, Maryland 20706
Hamilton Books Acquisitions Department (301) 459-3366

Estover Road
Plymouth PL6 7PY
United Kingdom

Printed in the United States of America
British Library Cataloging in Publication Information Available

Library of Congress Control Number: 2007942774
ISBN-13: 978-0-7618-3993-4 (paperback : alk. paper)
ISBN-10: 0-7618-3993-3 (paperback : alk. paper)

∞™ The paper used in this publication meets the minimum requirements of American National Standard for Information Sciences—Permanence of Paper for Printed Library Materials, ANSI Z39.48—1992

To my wife Cindy for incomprehensible loyalty and understanding beyond the scope of love and duty.

To Garrett and Taylor for accepting me into their childhoods and helping me put mine to rest.

Contents

Preface

Educational leaders have built the crumbling empire of public schools on foundational fallacies and misinterpretations, on the unquestioned premises that mirror adult society but emotionally cripple children, especially the children of abuse and neglect. These premises are never investigated, because they are based on assumptions that are so much a part of American culture that even the most distinguished leaders consider them to be human nature and not choice. Vouchers, fly-by-night quick fixes, political policy, careless funding, etc., are feeble attempts to patch the cracks that a century of historical and philosophical errors has created. Education reform must start by repairing the blueprints and not the leaky roof. Experts and consultants do not have the answers, for if they did, public school leaders would be focused on excellence instead of mediocrity. There would be no need for propaganda and manipulated data to convince the public all is well or the next idea will save the schools. They would be talking to the victims of educational inadequacies, not each other. The solution to most educational woes can be seen through the eyes that do not trust authority because authority has never been trustworthy to them. No human has a better perspective of where educational reform should begin more than the battered and belittled children of abuse. They have the biggest need for quality education and support. They need the extended families, the cooperative relationships, and the love that inspired educators to become educators. The experts are baffled because these are not the attributes of a leader who obtained power by surviving the obstacle course that defeats others in a society where competition is thought to build character and second place is not an option.

The size of this transparent subgroup is horribly underestimated because research involving abused children requires parental consent. Most cases are never detected or reported to under-funded governmental agencies that screen out nearly half of the reported abuse cases before inadequately investigating the rest. Recent accounts of these numbers, based on reflective surveys executed by adults, suggests that the population of abused and neglected children is as high as one in five children. These victims are forced to live by the misguided rules that underlie curriculum and policy. They are the children who are not being served by our schools because they do not fit into any identified subgroup for convenient labeling. They are the children who walk the halls undetected, anonymous shadows that gradually fade until they are neither forgotten nor remembered.

The solutions to the biggest problems facing education rest on the innocent tongues of the muted and unseen children of abuse. They are the champions who make this effort one of genuine hope, but for it to succeed, the heartbreaking stories contained within must be told. Data supports the philosophy, but no philosophy supports the data. No tables or graphs, just experience, the wisdom of the world's greatest thinkers, and a few children who touched my life are needed to bring to light the atrocities that systemically ignore the belittled and beaten on a daily basis. I feel that it is my duty and purpose to represent the submissive and confused children under the care of our educational networks. The situations presented in this book are very real and occurred during a five-year period. Names, settings, and physical descriptions were altered to protect identities, but I feel the personalities of the children were preserved.

The school has the power to cure their ills but has lost its focus and is more concerned with vocational training and national security. Aesthetic appreciation, the establishment of relationships, and intrinsic values are not tested, so they become unimportant. Therefore, the children who could possibly be saved by a nurturing climate are funneled into rows and taught repetition, obedience, and measurement. These desperate boys and girls, afraid to speak and unheard when they do, come to school seeking purpose and acceptance and find only unfair competition and rejection. Educators have the power to change this, not by spending or making new laws and policies, but by looking through their eyes. Experience their horrors and create safe havens that nurture, build relationships, and educate. And the beauty is, what nurses them benefits all, because what they need is what schools should be like anyway. Modify the blueprints, rebuild the foundation, and most every other problem disappears.

I honor the opportunity to represent the children who live in pain and emotional numbness. I hope that my unconventional approach serves abused children well. The children who are beaten and raped when others are doing homework. The children who do not strive, they cope. The children who are numb when they are not in tears. The children schools punish and fail. I know them because I have studied the issue from various perspectives. I know them because I have experience as a parent, teacher, educational leader, and professor. But most of all, I know them because I am one of them. I now honor the promises I made as a little boy nearly forty years ago.

Chapter One

A Face in the Crowd

"In some other life
I'll stand where I am standing now, and will look down, and will see
My own face, and not know what I am looking at."

—Charles Wright, "January" *Country Music*

MR. HATLEY'S CARPORT

Phillip was so familiar to the faculty he had achieved celebrity status at the tender age of 12. Like Elvis or Cher, his last name was never used in lounge discussions, but there was never any question as to which of the school's four children by that name was being referenced. I was new to the school and to school leadership, and it was only the end of August, but Phillip's antics had already reached legendary status although I had yet to meet him. I must admit that I had grown tired of the condescending looks I would get from teachers and the office staff when I confessed that I didn't know him; they treated me as if they were battle weary soldiers and I was the new recruit just joining the platoon. I was jealous of their experience and eager to prove to them that Phillip was just another child. I was also a little insulted. I had taught high school English for eleven years before accepting my first assistant principal job, so I was no stranger to discipline problems.

Our inevitable encounter soon followed. Phillip had cursed his teacher for taking his hat and was en route to the office to see me. I pulled a triplicated discipline form from my top drawer and positioned it neatly on my large calendar in the center of my enormous, oak desk. I heard mumbling outside my office door and then Sally, our secretary, responding in a pleasant voice that rang with gleeful anticipation, "Just one minute, Phillip. I will see if he is ready to see you!" She bounced into my office like a presenter at the Oscars, eager to give this moment its due introduction, but I cut her off and asked her to send him in. Her smile twitched and her eyes lost their glee, but she politely obliged.

The first thing I noticed was his expression, staring at me like a boxer facing his opponent at center ring before a title fight. His lip trembled and his black pupils peered curiously at me through squinted eyes. A black smudge graced his pale forehead and his brown hair was creased where his hatband fit his skull. His stained jeans were sagging below his butt and his worn sneakers were intentionally untied. He smelled like used motor oil. He plopped into one of the fabric chairs across from my desk and folded his nicked and bruised arms tightly across his stomach. Like gunslingers in the old West, we continued to gaze at one another, each waiting for the other to draw. I had seen him before, but I had no idea that *this* was the infamous sixth grader they call "Phillip."

As a rookie administrator, it occurred to me that my choice of discipline would be measured by the teachers who were still piecing together their opinion of me as an assistant principal. I could hear them in my mind, begging me to be strong and suspend him for as many days as the handbook would allow. I know because I was recently one of them, and likened myself to teachers more than administrators who seemed to have forgotten their humble beginnings. However, I felt as if the face before me could handle anything I had to offer. Even though I wore the tie and sat in the office chair behind the intimidating desk, he was obviously more familiar with his role than I with mine. Saturday school, in-school suspension, out-of-school suspension, and parent conferences—he could take anything in my holster. As I pondered into those darkened pupils it occurred to me that any playful, youthful quality one normally sees in children had been replaced by a grim view of his own existence. There was an angry numbness in his face that I have seen before in my brother. It was a numbness that had pervaded my own heart, an emptiness that I had learned to ignore when I was Phillip's age. Even though I had the power to disrupt his life for a brief period, I knew that I did not have the power to make a difference by following the guidelines established in the code of conduct.

"Phillip, I am Mr. Neal, the assistant principal. In a little bit I am going to discuss your behavior in Mrs. Cryer's class, but for now, I would like to talk to you. Are you ready to talk to me?" No answer. He fixed his eyes on my stapler and stared at it as if he expected it to explode at any moment. By this time, the sour odor of his clothes had become rather disturbing. His fingernails were blackened underneath, so I figured he must help work on cars.

"You like cars? Ever work on one?" Still no answer, but I did solicit a head shake. "No?" I had you pegged to be a guy who likes cars." Phillip shrugged his shoulders with his arms still folded across his middle. I paused, looking for another angle. There, beneath those stubby, scratched, and bruised arms, was the leg of a faded, screen-printed Spiderman, adorning the front of his powder blue, stretched tee shirt. Surely this would be all I needed because, as a child, I too loved Spiderman.

"Spiderman! I love Spiderman! I used to think he was the coolest superhero when I was a kid." He looked at me as if I were an idiot, but he wasn't grimacing, something I accepted as progress. "I thought he had the coolest costume. I still do. I just saw the movie this summer. Did you see it?" He did not answer, but he was looking at me now and he had unfolded his arms to occasionally glance at his shirt. I could see the rest of Spiderman now, swinging on a web. "He really was doing what he thought was right, but he was always misunderstood by the police and Mr. Jamison, you know, the editor of the newspaper. He didn't want people to know who he really was, so he wore a mask. As a child I was the same way. People didn't understand me and I wore a mask of sorts, because I wanted to be left alone. In a way, I think that is why I liked Spiderman. He was a little like me. Perhaps he was the only adult in my mind who could understand me, and he was only an imaginary character. I don't know. Is that why you like Spiderman?"

"Dis wuz my brudder's shirt," replied Phillip, plucking the hand-me-down as if he realized it was a worthless rag. My frustration mounted, but my determination to crack his exterior elevated as I regrouped from this setback. The fact that he spoke was comforting; his words were embellished with a speech impediment I obviously didn't anticipate. Then he grinned, exposing a tobacco-stained chipped tooth; he was apparently humored by my reaction. I got the feeling that every approach to reach him had been tried and he knew that I was walking down a familiar, dead-end path that many others had fruitlessly traveled. I decided to take a direct approach because I somehow sensed that I shared with him the source of his problems. I was rather certain I would be blazing a new trail of inquiry. It was a risk that perhaps required the brashness of a neophyte administrator.

"Whew! Those are some mighty big bruises," I stated, pointing toward his arms. "You must be a football player," even though I could tell he was no athlete. He glanced down at his forearms, and locked his elbows and rotated them while staring at each purple whelp like a sailor proudly scanning tattoos from distant ports. I noticed a swollen place just above his right elbow and saw scars I had not initially seen.

"Naw. I don't play no footbawl," he grinned proudly. "I wush I could, but I'd probly hurt somebody. Dey don't want none o' me." His face lost its anger as if he forgot who he was for a moment. He then, without further provocation, began telling me the story behind the bruises on his arms with the casual comfort of a lifelong buddy. "Ya see, d' udder day, me and Joey (his brother) got home from school off of da bus, you know, and we didn't have no key to get in, but dat wuz okay, because Maw Maw wuz inside d' trailer. We seen her feet on d' couch. She wuz sleepin'. So we knocked and knocked, but she didn't move none. Joey told me to go an' get Mr. Hatley, our neighbor who lets me an' Joey sleep in his carport when Dad and Maw Maw get too drunk or mad at us and stuff, 'cause he got a key. Anyway, he wuz gone, so den Joey told me dat we wuz gonna have to bust in the trailer door. I told him Maw Maw wuz probly just drunk, but he said she coulda had a heart attack or sumthin', so I thought about it for a minute, and he had a good point. I went to the steps and run across d' porch and hit d' door with my shoulder just like a football player. It took me two times, but I busted it in. Dat's why I said I'd hurt somebody if I played football."

"So that is how you bruised your arms?"

"Naw, man. Well, maybe a li'l bit. But dat happened when we busted d' door and den Maw Maw woked up later and started yellin' at us. She got a broom and started hittin' us, but I blocked it with my arms by holdin' dem over my head like dis." Phillip raised his palms above his forehead and placed the backs of his hands on his scalp. His elbows pointed at me as his forearms protected his nose. It occurred to me that she was trying to hit him in the face and head area because he obviously deflected the blows with his pudgy arms. "She busted the stick and throwed th' end piece at me. Den Daddy come in later on, mad as heck about d'door, home from drivin' his truck, and then Maw Maw showed him what all we done. He started hittin'me and Joey and we ran out. It was dark, so we went to Mr. Hatley's house and hid. He wuz gone, 'member? We spent d' night in d' carport. He got some old blankets and stuff dat he keeps out fer us and we use 'em 'cause he don't mind none."

I was a little shocked and saddened. I could envision each crack of the broomstick as it smacked the bone that ran from his elbow to his wrist. I saw the violence of his father's punches and the horrified look that must have been on Phillip and Joey's faces. And I could hear the high-pitched, frantic pleas for mercy and the outraged voices of adults, lost in frustration and life-long regrets. Phillip took me back to the hysteria that haunted my childhood in a matter of seconds. I pulled out my legal pad and solemnly began taking notes for what seemed like a minute but may have been twenty. As I replayed the images of my past that Phillip's story re-cultivated, I found myself revisiting the protective bower I built as a child. It is a quiet place where adults don't exist and accomplishments overcome shortcomings. Cruelty and suffering are temporarily silenced in this hideaway, only the voice of my inner child, who has always been there for me, can be heard. But I needed to understand Phillip at this moment, whose inner child might not be as helpful as mine seems to have been.

If this drama proved to be a recurring theme in Phillip's life, I realized that I needed to be careful at this point in our conversation. He was not reaching out for help when he explained his bruises; he was bragging. They were symbols of his toughness. To Phillip, the beating he described was not unusual or something he even considered unnatural. When dealing with an abused child, one never knows if and when he or she will inadvertently rub against that child's lamp, erroneously releasing the dark genie within. Perhaps I had done this. Phillip and his brother were leading barren lives where fear replaces love, insecurity dominates self-esteem, and shame consumes the human spirit. Phillip accepts abuse and rejection as normal aspects of each day. It is almost invisible to the adults in his community, but an experienced eye can detect it. Regardless, I had an opening and decided to pursue the answers to my questions, not knowing where my prodding would take him, or me.

"I played football. I didn't play when I was your age because I had a series of concussions. But I played when I was in high school. My eleventh grade year I had mono, got hit by a car (Phillip laughs), and pulled both groins, so I didn't play much. My senior year I was the county's leading pass receiver, which is good for a tight end, and earned a college scholarship. It was the best year of my life because it made me popular at school and gave me a lot of confidence."

"You got hit by a car? Wuz you walkin' or ridin'? Did it hurt?" I was a bit disappointed that he chose to completely discard my athletic accolades to focus on my inability to safely orchestrate what chickens seem to have perfected, even if only in classic riddles.

"Yes, I was walking across the street at night and a drunk driver was speeding through an intersection on the left side of the road and all I could do was jump into the air before it hit me. I saw the headlights lunging toward me and could hear the tires scream. Onlookers told me that he was going about 40 miles per hour at the time. It knocked off my shoes and the backs of my toes scraped the asphalt and my leg busted his headlight. When I slid up the hood, my head hit the windshield. I remember lying there, looking up into the black sky, as if the car was skidding in slow motion. I wondered if I would live. When the car finally rocked to a stop, I rolled off the front of the car and landed on my feet. The smell of smoldering rubber burned my nose. I stood, shoeless and stunned. Traffic had stopped and there were people there immediately to help me. My legs and toes hurt, but I walked away. Somebody who saw it said it would have killed me if I didn't jump just at the right time."

"Dat's cool! You musta been kinda tough when you wuz young!" Phillip nearly squealed as he smiled and then laughed. "How did ya land on your feet? Did ya just get lucky? I'd a had t' beat up dat drunk driver!"

I hesitated to give his comments some thought and to devise a way to get back on the topic. "At first I thought I was very lucky, but when I thought about it, I wasn't. I mean, do you think someone who gets hit by a Pontiac going 40 miles per hour is lucky? I really don't think there is luck. We all have things that happen to us, both good and bad. I didn't think about beating up the driver of the car. I didn't think he tried to hit me, even if he was on the wrong side of the road and drunk. He was a total stranger and whatever he did to me, I couldn't change by fighting him."

"I woulda knocked his head off!"

I thought I had found my angle. Trying to set him up using the Socratic method of questioning I became familiar with teaching senior English classes, he was now in my comfort zone. "Why would I want to beat him up?"

"Because, man, he coulda killed you."

"But he didn't."

Phillip became frustrated with my reasoning. "But he *coulda*!"

"Well, he didn't and I had no reason to get mad because he didn't know me or care about me."

"So! Dat don't matter. At least you coulda sued him or somethin'!"

"Would that have changed anything? I was okay, just sore for a few days. He didn't do it on purpose so it didn't hurt my feelings."

"Naw, but it woulda made me feel better to kick his butt or to sue him fer about a million dollars."

"Would you sue your Maw Maw or dad for breaking broomsticks over your arms or punching you?"

Phillip stopped for a moment. I was afraid that I crossed the line and he would withdraw. "Naw, but dat's differn't."

"How?"

Again Phillip paused. He looked at the stapler again for a while and rubbed his head from the nape of his neck over his face. "I dunno! It just is. You can't go 'round hittin' your folks and all. Dat ain't right. But dey can hit me 'cause I'm d' kid and dey d' grown ups."

I went for the checkmate, but I wasn't dealing with a normal pattern of logic when I appealed to Phillip. "So you think it is better for someone who is supposed to love you to hurt you on purpose than it is for a stranger to hurt you accidentally?"

I could tell by Phillips sober expression that I made the point. His pause was only for a second, but he squirmed and fidgeted in his chair as he pondered the question. He faked a grin and looked at his shoes and then again at my stapler, this time leaning forward and grabbing it to give it a closer inspection. Crouching over it as he held it in his hands that rested on his lap, he mumbled, "I dunno."

"Well I do," I quickly responded, starting to get angry as I pictured my new friend being beaten. "There are some people in the world who have a job to treat you fairly and care for you. I am one of those people and so are all the teachers here. Your Maw Maw and your dad are two others who are supposed to protect you. They are supposed to do that without hurting you."

Phillip looked disturbed. "Well, dey don't never do dat too much when dey ain't drinkin'. I look at it like dey ain't knowing exactly what dey mean to do when dey drunk. Dat's why we go to Mr. Hatley's mainly to get away from dem when dey drunk and mad. We know dey ain't comin' lookin' for us over there 'cause Mr. Hatley'll probly call da cops."

I went to open and close the door because it had become obvious that Sally and Ruby, the office workers, were perched right outside trying to listen in. Their normal pattern of muffled chatter had not been heard for some time now. When I returned to my seat, Phillip knew that I was upset, but there was a look in his eye that told me that he was happy that he was not the subject of my ire. He proceeded to tell me that his biological mother, a stripper with a drug habit, recently came by the trailer and stole "Rocky," their father's dog and Phillip's best friend. Phillip was afraid that she was going to train Rocky to fight in order to make money. I learned that his father drinks, smokes marijuana, and snorts cocaine when he can get it. Maw Maw sticks to beer, but when she drinks she gets very violent until she passes out. I asked Phillip if he would mind writing down these things so I can get some help for him. He told me that he couldn't write and he didn't need any help because that would only make things "worser."

"Phillip, I know how you feel because my childhood was not much different. My mother drank, filled the house with smoke, and shouted cuss words at me for little to no reason. I was slapped until bloody slobber flew from my mouth and beaten so badly the purple and scabbed lash marks stayed for weeks afterwards. I recall once being hit in the face with a fly swatter because I was laughing at the dinner table. I think my mother loved me, just not when I was around."

"My mudder don't care nothin' about us. She just cares about getting' high. Dad, he's da one dat loves us, I reckon."

"What about Maw Maw? Is she you grandmother?"

(Laughing) "Naw, she ain't really nuthin'. She's somebody Dad found on a run and brung her home to cook and clean for us while he's gone on d' road. We call her dat because she don't want us callin' her Mom or Mama or stuff like dat. I started calling her Maw, but she got mad, so we call her Maw Maw now. I don't think she likes it cuz we called her dat to make her mad until one day it just stucked. She don't think about it no more."

"Phillip, how long has she lived with you?"

"Well, at dis trailer she lived with us fer about six or nine weeks. At d' udder trailer she lived wid us just a few weeks until we got kicked out and moved to d' new trailer over at Mr. Hatley's house."

"Why were you kicked out?"

"I dunno. Probly cuz she left out and stayed gone and wouldn't come home until Dad was comin' home. Joey and me wuz on our own most d' time."

"Why didn't you tell somebody. There are people here at school. . ."

"Mr. O'Neal! Would you tell somebody if you wuz a kid? We had d' best fun ever! We wuzn't tellin' nobody!"

Phillip explained that the owner of the trailer park came by a few times to collect rent and noticed that the kids were unsupervised. He called the sheriff, but the only result was a threat of eviction. Mr. Hatley is a man who worked with Phillip's father. His mother or grandmother had lived in a trailer behind his house until she passed away, so he agreed to rent it out.

I had broken through to Phillip, and a small sense of accomplishment lifted my pity and caused me to temporarily believe that I could succeed where countless others before me had failed. With the surprise of Arthur as he felt Excaliber sliding from its stone sleeve, I felt unprepared for the responsibility of this new power. I was convinced that Phillip was reaching to me for help, or that he had always been reaching towards adults incapable of helping. His face had lost the hardness and the scowl, but now he lacked the confidence to look me in the eye, especially when his rambling ventured onto sensitive side streets. His strong Southern drawl and his speech impediment had become hardly noticeable, but for some reason I couldn't take my eye from the dirty smudge on his white, lightly-freckled forehead. Because I was involved in reading *The Sorcerer's Stone* with my oldest child every evening, it was natural to compare the dirt mark to Harry Potter's scar. Perhaps both were symbols of a personal triumph over the vicious nature of some adults.

It occurred to me that I would have to report Phillip's story to the Department of Social Services, and I couldn't help but feel that it would betray him. In Phillips words, his confidence in me would only make things "worser." I had to call his father anyway because Phillip and Joey, who was in the eighth grade, each owed over $20 to the cafeteria and neither had completed an application for free and reduced lunch. We had inactive phone numbers and notes and letters home solicited no response. My first impulse was to get to Dad and let him know, in so many words, that I was going to be watching Phillip and his brother very carefully, and if he or Maw Maw continued to abuse them I would be all over the situation. I try not to be a very complicated person, so I decided to go with my first impulse, before I had a second. I was going to visit Phillip's dad, with free-lunch form and receipt book in hand and a much more significant agenda behind my back. However, Phillip was still in my office and there needed to be closure.

"Phillip, I had better not see you in here again because you won't take a stupid ball cap off your head. I better not have to deal with you because you are giving one of these teachers a hard time. You need to learn to read and write instead of running around here like some kid who wants to work at McDonalds all his life." It occurred to me that my example might not have much effect on Phillip since he probably considers such a position in the dynamic fast-food industry as one of considerable prestige, but I continued. "I told you a little bit about my childhood. I am not different from you. I think that you are a victim of child abuse until you are old enough to do something about it. If you still accept it, you are not a victim but an accomplice to your own demise. I realize that you don't know what that means but. . ."

"Yes I do, Mr. O'Neal. My uncle is a complice. He's in prison, well, he wuz or maybe he still is, I dunno."

"Then you get the idea," I responded, reminded of three of my relatives, all current or former products of the North Carolina correctional system. It was then an empty realization came over me. My father worked nights when I was younger, and my mother was an alcoholic who, at times, was vicious to my younger brother, sister, and me. Sometimes I would go all week without seeing Dad, and when I did, Mom had a list of things we had done wrong over the past five days. He often greeted us with a Friday night or Saturday morning belt whipping. It occurred to me that the smudgy, illiterate, lisping boy with the Southern drawl, bad haircut, and no self-esteem who was sitting in my office hot seat, was me.

DADDY DEAREST

As mentioned, I escaped the horrors of my childhood by creating a mental and psychological bower, a retreat where I entered an imaginary place where I communed with the very real and reasonable voices of my inner child. Phillip possibly did not have this capability, so he and his brother found Mr. Hatley's carport. The more I thought about it, the more sobering it became. I asked Phillip when his father would be home again, and he told me that he was home at that moment. I explained to him that I was going to visit the trailer to take him some lunch forms to complete. He became confused, as if he had a premonition of his two fragile worlds colliding.

"Now Phillip, I am not going to give you an I.S.S. (in-school suspension) or send you home for a day, but I need your word that you will come see me the next time you feel smothered by teachers or Maw Maw or whatever. I am going to try to help you, but I need you to trust me. I will do everything I can to make things better for you and not 'worser'." I don't think he believed me, or he had no idea what I was talking about. Either way, he shook my hand when I offered it, took the pass I had written for him, and stood to leave. As he turned, his face recaptured his trademark scowl and he headed back out into the school.

Going to his father's house, my mind randomly recalled the time when I was about six years old my teenage uncle held me down and spat in my face repeatedly much to his and his friends' amusement. He was seven years older so I was rather helpless, but I never forgot it. Since I was afraid of adults and making the problem "worser," I didn't tell on him or seek sanctuary in my mother's arms, I retreated into my bower. I vowed that I would get him back one day. When I finally became big enough to confront him about it, I did nothing. Sometimes I regret not doing the same thing to him, but I imagine he would not have remembered the incident and I would have felt like a crazed lunatic (by normal standards), even though such behavior is nothing extraordinary in my family. I had already begun my separation from the character flaws of my lineage, so I began the process of "relative extinction" in lieu of "interfamilial revenge." He was off my list, no longer kin, even if his contaminated blood had properties that were linked to my own. There were numerous other incidents that incrementally increased the distance between us, but none where I was his victim. By then I knew that he had a drug problem and I was beginning to see the relationship between cruelty and mind-altering substances. I grew to realize that we are ever-changing creatures, different people in one evolving frame, sharing the others' experiences. Seeking self-gratifying revenge for something that occurred when I was six would signify nothing, except that he contributed to the stunting of my growth into a dignified human being. Several years later and rather climactically, he was imprisoned for trying to kill a man with a hammer; although in fairness to him and the accuracy of this reflection, I am not sure if it was a claw or ball pein.

Instead of going after the people who abused me, I have found it to be more productive and fulfilling to go after the offenders of other children. What I did not anticipate was the number of abused children I would find in such a short period of time—inadvertent encounters—such as my run-in with Phillip Gregg.

The mobile home was worse than I imagined it. Even though it sat on level ground, the illusion was as if it were about to roll down a hill. The cinderblocks beneath the home were exposed and adorned with dirt-dobber nests reddened by the Carolina clay. These same blocks were cleverly stacked to form the front steps that led to a small, home-made porch near the front door. Cardboard window replacements backed broken glass panes and there was orange and brown rust in areas where many seasons of rain had drained from the roof of this narrow domicile. The storm door had no glass or screen, but guarded the prefabricated front door as if it had some unknown purpose. It had lost its recoil spring, but had been repaired with an orange, elastic cord. I knocked, not sure whether I should stand erect when I entered or lean with the trailer. I heard a muffled groan coming from within that I could only assume was an acknowledgement, a primal response to my request to enter. I listened to the creaks and thuds of someone walking to the front door. There was the thump of the deadbolt being unlocked and the chain of the other lock jingled as it slid to the opening on the other side, and then it was dropped, clinking against the interior wall. The door cracked open and a squinting eye poked out at me. It was then I noticed that, when closed, the door was being held up by the deadbolt and one hinge. Without the support of the lock, it wavered unsteadily in the hands that belonged to the eye.

"Uh huh?" came a voice from behind that bloodshot eye, nestled in a fat, unshaven cheek.

"Mr. Gregg? I am Gerry Neal, assistant principal at the middle school. I have some paperwork that has to be signed today and I need to discuss another matter with you, if you don't mind. I realize you are busy and I won't take up very much time."

"What kind of paperwork?"

"Just some forms from the cafeteria manager."

The door opened and he grabbed it with both hands to stabilize it as I entered. "Damn boys done torn up m' door knockin' 'gainst it like a couple sorry-ass bulls. S'cuse the mess." The trailer was indeed as it appeared, leaning toward the front door. The smell was horrendous, like he had been cooking cabbage all morning, but there was nothing on the stove. I remember it being very dark on the inside, even after my eyes adjusted from the sunlight. I sat in the frayed fabric couch across from an old, floor-model television with a greenish picture. The excitement of a game show blurted noise into the room as he plopped into a duct-taped chair beside me. The only thing worse than the cabbage smell was his ripe body odor. Before I handed him the free and reduced lunch cafeteria form, he wiped his hands on his grimy, wife-beater tee shirt as if I was bestowing upon him a sacred artifact. As soon as he recognized the form, he said to me rather indignantly, "I done filled one a' dem out. Dey said I make too much money to get free lunches."

"Then we have a problem. Both of your boys owe the cafeteria a good bit of money."

"Naw, dat ain't right. I give Ginger money to put on their account every time before I make a run. Dey ain't no way!"

"Who is Ginger?" I asked him as I gradually noticed empty, folded beer cans on the coffee table and the floor around it.

"She da lady who rears my kids when I ain't here. She been livin' wid us fer a while now."

"You mean Maw Maw?" As soon as I asked I knew that was a stupid question. Any man of even limited intelligence would know that I had been talking to Phillip or Joey about somewhat personal matters. I also remembered that she didn't like that name, so it may be offensive to him as well. Fortunately, those thoughts passed him by like a feather in a windstorm and he just laughed.

"She ain't here or I'd get her in here to straighten dis thang out. I give her ten dollars for bof of dem boys last Mondey. She gone into town now to get somethin' in my truck."

I decided to drop the bomb. "Mr. Gregg, Phillip was sent to my office today because he keeps acting up in school. When he. . ."

"You just let me know whenever he does. I'll whoop his ass. He ain't none too old to get a ass whoopin'. Dat boy ain't been nothin' but. . ."

I returned the interruption. "That is why I am here. You and I grew up in a time when child beatings were considered normal, none of anybody's business. But today. . ."

"Bible says; 'spare d' rod, spoil d' child.'"

I always thought it was funny how some people use the Bible to justify their actions instead of using it as a guide. As an educator, however, I left that one alone. He didn't know the origin of the cliché anyway. "Today we are learning about the long-term effects of child abuse." I figuratively slapped myself for being so stupidly direct.

"Hey! Now wait just a damn minute. Nobody here said nothin' 'bout no child abuse. There's a difference, and you ain't gonna come in my. . ."

"Mr. Gregg, would you hear me out. I am not going to sit here and try to come up with an agreeable definition of child abuse with you!" I felt like I was out of time because he was angrily attempting to stand, but was having difficulty getting out of the chair while showing me that he was offended. "I will tell you one thing. I have examined Phillip's arms and he described to me what has been going on." Getting louder to be heard over his attempts to interrupt and throw me out, I continued, "If I see it again and I *will* check, I will not only call D.S.S. on you, I will call the sheriff!"

"Fine, you said what you had to say! now get d' hell out of my house or I will call da law on *yur* ass!" I left quickly, probably because the front door was downhill from the couch, and there was the possibility that he might have a gun or something. However, I figured he probably didn't own one or Phillip and his brother would already be full of more holes than a slab of Wisconsin Swiss. He caught the unsupported door as I released it into his hand. I jumped over the cinderblock steps out into the tall pasture grass surrounding my car and quickly fumbled for my keys. It had not gone as I would have planned, but then again, I really didn't have a plan. I didn't know if my actions constituted harassment or not, but if they did not, then I didn't do it correctly.

As I wheeled the car around and headed through the field back to the road, I passed what had to be Mr. Hatley's small, frame house. I looked at the attached carport with extreme solemnity, as if it were an out-of-place war memorial stuck in the middle of a rural Southern county. I had envisioned it to be at least a few hundred yards from the trailer, but it was only about fifty feet from the trailer's front porch. There was a path of round, cement slabs that led from the porch to the house, something I didn't notice driving up. I imagined the boys fleeing down that walkway from the drunken yelling inside the trailer finding safe harbor under the roof of that carport, between the utility room and the old pickup that was parked there as I rode by. I felt guilty for what I might have just done to Phillip, which amounted to nothing more than stirring a hornet's nest above his head. I wasn't sure whether I had acted selfishly or on Phillip's behalf, but I meant every word. I was determined to stop him and Maw Maw. I returned to school and refined my documentation. The Department of Social Services asked their standard questions. They informed me that they were going to review the information to determine if an investigation would be an appropriate course of action.

The following day Mr. Gregg appeared in the office. He was dressed much nicer than before and had bathed and shaved, so I barely recognized him. He told the secretary that he was there to pay the lunch debt, and he did just that. I felt that I just couldn't let him slip away, so I sarcastically asked him if he intended to pay some money in advance or if he was under the impression that we operate on a credit plan. He gave me a blank stare, and then laughed as if he pitied me, shaking his balding head and stuffing the receipt into his pants pocket. He looked at me and said calmly, "Can we talk?" I nodded and invited him into my office.

He sat in the same chair his son had occupied less than 24 hours earlier, with the same scowl and apparently the same familiarity with the principal's office. He looked at me and exhaled forcefully. "Look, me and you got off to a bad start. I ain't like you think I am. But I got it tough 'cause da boys ain't got no real mama to speak of, when she ain't out whorin' or doin' drugs she ain't out. An' Ginger she's hard on Joey 'n Phillip 'cause she ain't used to takin' care of no kids, 'specially dem two. Dey ain't give her a chance 'cause dey think she ain't stayin' around long, but she wants to stay. Anyhow, I guess its my fault dat dey act like dey do, but dey ain't gonna listen to a bunch of talk or being grounded. Dem two only knows one language and dat's d' only one I know'd growin' up. I just don't want to see 'em goin' to jail an' all."

I hesitated, reminding myself to act on Phillip's behalf. "You know, Mr. Gregg, you act like it is important for me to understand why you treat those boys the way you do. It is not about you. I am only concerned for your boys. If you threaten them or hurt them, then you are something I never will understand or ever want to understand."

"Well, dem boys is exaggeratin' more times dan not. Ginger'll tell you dat much."

I looked him in the eye and said, "Mr. Gregg, I reported Phillip's bruises to D.S.S. and gave them information he told me during a conversation we had for nearly an hour yesterday. I took several pages of notes and faxed them to the caseworker. I should tell you that I will do the same after this conversation."

Mr. Gregg's chin fell to his chest. He slapped his thighs and rocked out of his seat and left, nearly bumping into a teacher on her way into my office. Mrs. Cryer, the self-contained exceptional children's teacher, closed the door behind her while looking back at Mr. Gregg. Her expression quickly told me that she was upset. "Mr. Neal, I realize that you are busy and have a lot to do, but I have a concern." Her eyes pierced mine as her aging face trembled in a weak effort to restrain her anger. "Phillip wore a different hat today and I suppose he thinks we are going to go easy on him like we did yesterday. He has been warned and warned about his clothes, hats, not doing his homework, and I think he needs some serious consequences!"

"Like O.S.S. (Out-of-School Suspension)?"

"Well, yes. He won't come to Saturday school and can't stay after school. I.S.S. needs a break from him once in a while, and quite frankly, so do we!"

"We?"

"Mrs. Gamble (her teaching assistant) and me. Come on, Mr. Neal. We need consistency and he needs discipline. He is laughing at us. If we don't set the tone early in the year, the problem is just going to get worse. I don't mean to tell you how to do your job, but I feel that I am experienced and professional enough to come in here and let you know what many of the teachers think about the situation."

I understood her frustration, but it was nothing compared to Phillip's. Every adult in his life, every woman and man charged with his development have bullied him and tried to discard him. She did not understand that

Phillip's behavior was a reaction, a response to the anguish and the raping of dignity and confidence that he endures daily. There is no place where Phillip is accepted by the adult world. There are no detention halls that will meet his needs, no special classrooms or Saturday punishments. Modifications or medications are not the answer either. Mrs. Cryer failed to realize that she was not offering what he needed—opportunity, kindness, and patience. Confinement is counterproductive to a child who needs relationships and success to prosper. So Phillip improvises when he finds solace on the oil-stained cement in Mr. Hatley's carport, a place where frustrated adults ignore him and he can be himself. It is his bower, where his inner child consoles him, kisses his bruises, and covers him with canvas tarps to protect him from the frigid darkness that engulfs him. I had no reply that would quickly appease Mrs. Cryer, so I advised her to take the hat, give it to me, and I would keep it until the end of the year. Her reaction suggested that this was not the answer she wanted to hear. She left to continue her campaign against my decisions by immediately reporting my insensitivities to the torch and pitchfork-bearing mob congregated in the teacher's lounge.

My experience with Phillip unlocked rooms that had been unvisited for years. Every punch, slap, lash, and harsh word chips away at the child's sense of normalcy and his self image. The belittlement is so severe in many cases, the child usually blames himself for his own inadequacies and fears. Childhood and adolescence are awkward times when we define who we are and design what we will become. Success in school requires confidence, an ability to take chances, and a willingness to try again because the child's support system is in tact. When that support is a series of degrading and painfully negative acts that reinforce the concept of failure, the child will not take the chances that coincide with proper social, cognitive, and even physical development. This is consistent with what I have read, but this realization did not come from a book. In many ways it came from Phillip and the way he opened the darkened chambers of my past.

My interaction with the legendary boy extracted so much personal anguish that I thought had long been forgotten. The rusted locks on the iron doors that line the shadowy and bleak corridors of my youth were released, and the ghosts of banished memories floated back and screamed through my skull. One by one, I paralleled his stories with mine, matching each of his horrors with a nightmare of my own. I heard the cries for mercy and the snapping sound of leather cracking into the soft skin of a child. I felt the sting of the slaps and the throbbing of blood rushing to the area where he had been punched. I sensed fear swelling in his stomach and throat, and I could see, through the watery scope of tear-filled eyes, the reddened and angry face of a grown man delivering endless blows. I heard so much defenseless screaming and felt so much unnecessary pain. I re-experienced the frantic blur of violence as my mind's eye saw him scrounging for safety on the floor like a gun-shy hound being brutally trained by his master. Yet my only recourse was to act in a manner that would risk more abuse and not guarantee that his needs would be met. According to the law, I had no choice.

Chapter Two

Brethren

> "Denial of human dignity discredits the worth of any cause that needs such denial to assert itself. And the suffering of just one child discredits that worth as radically and completely as does the suffering of millions."
>
> —Zygmunt Bauman, *Liquid Love*

THE FOOTBALL STAR AND THE MILITARY BRAT

My father was a nineteen-year-old freshman football player at the University of South Carolina who had just married his high school sweetheart, eighteen, when he learned that they were expecting a child, despite having been told that a childhood Jeep accident made my mother incapable of bearing children. Dad seemed to have escaped an abusive upbringing through athletics, and was proud to be the first person in the family ever to have completed high school. Sports would be his ticket out of the poverty of a small town amidst the tobacco fields in eastern North Carolina, and the means by which the battering and cruelty at the hand of his step-father would only have an ephemeral impact on his life, at least from outsiders' perspectives. He became a high school superstar in his hometown and outgrew the abuse of his step-father, as strangers who align themselves with winning athletic programs showed him love and admiration.

Mom was basically a chain-smoking military brat, a colonel's daughter, who fell in love with the local sports icon. Her Oregonian family was a bit imbalanced, probably the result of hateful arguments that were brutally personal and emotionally crippling. She, her mother, and sister were elitists for the most part, conditioned to believe that their actions were not to be questioned by enlisted personnel or other commoners. Mom's father had little to do with her upbringing; there are times when some men find war more inviting than family, I suppose. Regardless, Mom's family opposed her marriage to what they believed to be a hick from North Carolina, son of a drunken wife beater and unwanted stepson to an abusive truck driver from an impoverished coal town in West Virginia.

These are the ingredients that produced the embryo that can be traced to the man sitting at his computer over forty years later, recalling his childhood with sorrow and a nostalgic numbness in an effort to intrinsically discover the link between child abuse and resiliency. Since I now have a doctorate degree and my home's value is no longer calculated by factoring in mileage, an outsider might think I have a solid pedigree, but the mutts that my parents produced were cursed from their first gasps of earthly air. I inherited from my mother her addictive qualities and bipolarity. From my father, I was issued the athletic shoes I could never fill. All of these attributes would affect my life at different times. Because the bipolar and addictive tendencies didn't manifest themselves until adulthood, the casual observer might think that I was saved from this disposition. I was a successful athlete (by others' standards) and my grades were above average. Nonetheless, I had hardly escaped my fate; in fact, I would eventually be blindsided. The design was complete and this would be my blueprint, the genetic platform on which the quiet desperation of my childhood and beyond would play out.

One might assume that I had it better than Phillip because I was raised in a two-parent, middle-class family. In some ways I did, but there were many times I would have been envious of Phillip's situation, particularly when Maw Maw was not around. Having two parents meant that I was twice as likely to receive a beating, although I learned rather quickly that the participants in this tag-team duo were quite different. Dad was the executioner while Mom served as the sniper. When we had committed a major crime and the beating was to be severe, Dad would be waiting, swinging his looped, limber belt into his opposite, open hand. Mom's area of expertise was the quick hit with no prefacing speech that included our accusation and sentence. It was largely dependent upon her mood, so there were usually warning signs that hinted she was about to strike, but not always.

When I was about nine, I walked up behind her in the kitchen after my brother or sister had irritated her, probably repetitiously asking her when dinner would be served; it was late and we were all hungry. I unknowingly asked her the same question, and she whirled around and hit me with open hand square in the left ear, rocking the side of my head to the right, causing me to lose my balance. I fell toward the range, catching myself cleanly, except for the fact that my right hand landed on a vacant, red-hot burner. It sizzled and smoked in the fraction of a second I left it there before yanking it back and continuing my fall, which led to my chin being split open on an extended knife drawer. I hit the floor, screaming and holding my fried fingers as the blood from my face poured into the cradled hand. A high-pitched ringing deafened my left ear. Pain from the burn was shooting up my arm into my spine. "Get up, you whining little bastard!" she yelled, admittedly before she knew the extent of her damage. "You're not hurt!" Once she realized that I had indeed suffered injuries, she lectured me, while she doctored my wounds, about sneaking up on her. For the remainder of my childhood, I do not recall ever asking her when dinner would be served again.

Dad, on the other hand, was the victim of very cruel and merciless beatings when he was a youth. They lasted until he became big and brave enough to fight back. We never reached that pinnacle because the physical element waned before we matured, although the emotional abuse and neglect remained. I am sure that Dad never considered his brand of discipline to be abusive, because his method was much more controlled than the violence he endured. He would enter the room with his "belt" in hand, a thin strap of flexible leather that probably hadn't been threaded through a pair of pants since the Truman administration. In fact, it was always dangling in his closet like a hangman's noose on the village gallows, a disturbing yet constant reminder for all who passed that there was a darkness within capable of sapping the humanity out of the entire house in a matter of seconds. He would yell at us, words we never comprehended because we were futilely crying and fervently rubbing the backs of our bare legs as if the friction would toughen them. Fear swelled where remorse for our actions should have been, but we knew the routine that preceded the beatings. The pain of each lash of the belt was so intense it made my ears pop and eyes tingle. It is traumatic for a child to watch a hero transform into a monster and attack him in his own bedroom. Dad's face would turn red and the veins and tendons in his athletic neck would protrude. Through tightened, angered lips, he'd grunt with each mighty swing of his leathery lance. So we would jump, curl into fetal positions, cover our faces, and shriek. The fury, in a room where justice, dignity, and compassion were merely words to be applied to another place and time, was barbaric.

The slamming of our cheap, hollow door signaled the end of the beatings. Looking back, I can say that I never knew if he took mercy on us or just became fatigued by the energy that an all-out attack required. The room suddenly had the somberness of Gettysburg's aftermath—soundless, save the muffled whimpers of the wounded. I remember easing into my bottom-bunk and covering myself with the cool cotton sheets, the lash marks still burning deep into my tender flesh. In the midst of hard weeping, I gasped for air and spit the salty tears from my mouth, staring blankly into the semi-transparent meshing covering the underside of my brother's box springs above. The makeshift canopy was not enough to protect me from invading forces, but it cradled me until I could rise again, venture out of the room, and face the next challenge of my childhood. It must have been my bower before I learned to internalize one, an imaginary gauntlet where I learned to cope. It was my carport, I suppose, where I made promises to my adult self, the promises that would break the cycle of abuse in my lineage, and, perhaps, the promises that would silently guide me into the field of education.

FAMILY TIES

There is a very subtle scene in the Walt Disney animated film entitled *The Lion King*[1] that caught my attention when I was watching it with Taylor and Garrett, my two sons, a few years ago. Mufasa, the large, male lion, king of the pride lands, is very upset with his son Simba, a curious cub who had ventured far from safety, directly disobeying his father's direct order. Characterized by the powerful and deep voice of James Earl Jones, an angry Mufasa thunders to Simba, "COME HERE!" Simba drops his head and slowly approaches the giant lion from behind. He stumbles upon Mufasa's huge footprint, sculpted into the mud of the Savannah plain. Ever so gently, he places his tiny paw into the molded track, revealing his miniscule stature in comparison to that of his father. His fearful and moist eyes look up drearily toward his dad, who sits firm and rigid, his huge, muscular back and flowing mane towering over the scolded cub. Eventually, Simba's slow cadence stops at the feet of the great predator, whose face is stern and rigid with anger. Simba looks up into his father's eyes, ready to accept his inevitable punishment. But when Mufasa finally breaks the silence, his concerned voice is surprisingly gentle and loving. After his fatherly lesson is delivered, they play and laugh in the tall grass on their way back home. It is a powerful message, one that so eloquently and laconically addresses the issue of child abuse.

Children look to the adults in their lives for love, support, and guidance. When they reach out for these things and receive anger, ridicule, and neglect, the implications are traumatic and lasting. Adults hurt children in many ways, many times without intending to do so. They are angry or frustrated and the child appears at the wrong moment and becomes the object of the adult's inabilities to cope with his or her own stressors. Ironically, the source of that frustration often stems from deeply seeded and ancient episodes of abuse that older adults inflicted upon them when they were children. Although there are various forms and combinations of abuse that carry with them similar and different mental consequences, all of them have a profound impact on various levels of development in children.

Philip Ney, Tak Fung, and Adele Wickett determined in a study that investigated the various forms of child abuse (physical, verbal, emotional, sexual, and neglect) that less than five percent occur singly, without another form.[2] Therefore, one could easily generalize that, in most cases, there will be the presence of another form of abuse. Their labors investigated the combinations that have the most detrimentally profound impact on the child. It is nearly impossible to have any form of physical abuse without emotional abuse, but it can occur. As a former victim, it is my contention that the emotional abuse is far more destructive than anything physical, even, in some cases, where death is the result. At least in the case of death, there is no emotional abuse. At least there is mercy, just not from the hand of the abuser.

Looking back at Phillip, there were signs of more forms of abuse than merely physical. The fact that his head was dirty and he occasionally slept in a carport strongly suggests that he was physically neglected. Witnessing his caretakers' drug and alcohol problems and their seemingly unaffectionate approaches toward Phillip point toward emotional neglect. I would later discern that Phillip was educationally neglected when he moved into a new school district and there was never a request for transcripts; apparently, Dad and Maw Maw forgot to enroll him and he missed several weeks. There was little doubt that he experienced both verbal and physical abuse. I have no reason to do more than speculate about possible sexual abuse because he did not display the subtle signs that are indicative of a child who might be suffering from that particular affliction. It is important to note that the role of the educator is to recognize suspected abuse and report it, leaving the diagnosis to the professionals.

BUS 355

On a Valentine's Day several years ago, a school bus driver brought two children into my office, a boy and a girl, because they had been engaged in a fistfight when the bus arrived to pick them up earlier that morning. As the assistant principal, it would be my job to hear the details and dole out the punishment. The children had lived together for about a year, since the boy's father moved in with the girl's mother. They referred to themselves as brother and sister, even though there was obviously no blood relation. Both seventh graders were seemingly very angry when they plopped into the blue, fabric-covered chairs in my office, purposely placed several feet apart for moments such as this. Strangely, they calmed down quickly, before I could tell them to do so, and both smiled embarrassingly at me.

As the routine interrogation began, I was surprised that they did not show anger toward one another, considering the driver had to separate them just ten minutes earlier. They were courteous, respectful, and understanding; I sensed that their bitterness was real, but not aimed at anyone in the room. It occurred to me that something must have happened, something beyond their control that caused them to turn on one another. Initially I figured that the problem was gossip as it often can be with middle schoolers, "he said, she said" stuff that tends to send early adolescent lives into various degrees of chaos. Eventually, however, I sensed urgency in their voices that told me this was going to be a long story with no simple solution. Perhaps this problem was real; they seemed to be competing with one another for my attention. After three or four minutes, I knew that there was an issue that would come bubbling up that would make this inquiry far from routine. I had no idea of the magnitude.

"Starla, what did David say to you that made you mad enough to fight him?" No reply, but she looked at David and forced a sheepish grin. Her red hair was pulled back into a ponytail that seemed to accentuate her rather large, freckled nose; she wore a white t-shirt that was a size too small, exposing a prematurely developed figure. I figured that the best way to get to the root of the problem would be to re-enact the verbal exchanges, where many assistant principals might go straight to the more severe infractions, the physical aspects of the altercation. David, a student whose name is synonymous with delinquency and off-task behavior, much like Phillip, found the words much more easily. In fact, it seemed that he found them rather proudly. He leaned forward to speak.

"I called her a bitch and a whore," he said matter-of-factly, and sat back and folded his arms and looked at me as if I would most certainly agree. His voice was deeper than other 13-year-old students, and his face was stern and troubled. Rarely was the area between his eyebrows without wrinkles from squinting at the world around him, a bitter grimace that had become his routine expression. His eyebrows pushed even closer together and the wrinkles deepened as he prepared to speak again. "I told her she was a whore 'cause she slept with her father," he added, as if to provide the damning evidence that would help convince me that his previous comment was justified.

Starla lashed back in a blood-curdling attack, "I did not! That was my sister! And don't act like you ain't done some stuff what I could say about you!" David looked ashamed and confused. Instantly his expression changed and he became silently defensive, as if already contemplating when to raise the surrender flag. His oily bangs partially covered bluish-green eyes that were like turbulent seas before a storm. Fear replaced certainty in them, as he seemed to kneel like a defeated warrior succumbing to his inevitable slaughter at the hand of his victorious foe. I expected more of a fight, but Starla was the smarter of the two, so he was no match for her without the threat of violence to keep her within check. She locked in a threatening stare, as if the slightest draft in the room would push her to act. They gazed at each other. She figuratively circled him, sadly gloating over her triumph before administering the fatal blow, but one that would prove to be just as damaging to her the moment it was delivered. The cadence of time stalled as she froze, anticipating her next move and analyzing its consequences. Her brown eyes widened at David. "I'll tell him about Uncle Steve," she whispered in a prophetic tone so soft her mild lisp was unnoticeable. Her sword struck its mark and his head dropped into his hands. There was no mistaking that she had won this little argument. She had just played her trump card and there was no turning back.

David looked up at me through pooling tears and tried to gasp for enough air to form words. Starla seemed to feel uncomfortably satisfied that she had silenced him and leaned back, never breaking her trance-like stare. Then David told me words I will never forget and perhaps the words that would have the most dramatic impact on his life to that point. He muttered, "Uncle Steve one time made me suck on his growing." At first, I was confused, I did not understand because there was an emotional outburst through his tears that distorted his enunciation. Eventually, however, the horror of his meaning struck me with such force that the glowing florescent rods above my desk were not strong enough to withhold the sudden darkness that momentarily blurred my sight. My heart bounced in my stomach as I conditioned my face to reveal nothing of the hysteria inside. A heavy chill ran up my back and nested at the nape of my neck. It was the one form of abuse that I avoided. I can only imagine the degree of courage and shame that pulsed through his lips when those words formed.

He and Starla told me that when they were "bad," Uncle Steve would take off his pants and whip them with a belt until they both performed sexual acts on him or on one another while he watched, telling each what to do. Starla described an attempted rape in a nearby park where she had to run over a mile to a nearby restaurant to call for help. She told me that he made her strip and fondled her breasts and genitalia, but she fled when he tried to penetrate her. David explained how Uncle Steve had been accused of sodomizing his older brother (who then attended the high school) and how he too was forced to perform various acts that gave Uncle Steve sexual gratification. When they started talking, words flowed out of their mouths as if they were in a competition to purge their souls of the guilt that consumed them. My note taking could not keep up; I had to calm them because they were talking at the same time. I was in shock and having difficulty with the perfunctory aspects of my duties, as rage and pity periodically stunned my pen. I calmed them once I had control of myself and decided what to say to them. I do not remember what it was, but they were placed in separate rooms until I had developed a course of action.

I immediately called a Department of Social Services (DSS) Child Protective Services (CPS) caseworker, and was told that they would review the details and let me know if they would accept the case. The caseworker, Angie, called back and explained some of the family history to me so we could protect the students from those who might harm them further. She probably broke confidentiality laws to do so, but sometimes it is important to decide whose rights should be protected and act accordingly. Starla's biological father was accused of raping her older sister, and there is reason to believe Starla also; he was denied visitation unless other adults were present. One year earlier, Uncle Steve had been accused of sodomizing David's older brother, now in high school, but the charges were either dropped for unknown reasons or were still pending. Steve did not live with the two children, but Starla and David were dropped off at his home for the weekend occasionally. The caseworker said she would investigate the parents for neglect because they had knowledge of Uncle Steve's past exploits, at least the accusations against him, but continued to take their children to him for prolonged visits. She added that they would not classify this particular situation as an emergency because the children were not presently living with the accused. Someone would be out to question Starla and David within a few weeks, to determine if their parents were neglectful as mentioned. Angie called me back about fifteen minutes later to tell me that Uncle Steve is actually no relation to the family, that the children called him that because he requested it several months prior to the events on that particular Valentine's Day. Much in the same manner they called one another brother and sister or Phillip rather mockingly called his hitchhiking nanny "Maw Maw," I have noticed that desperate children from broken homes tend to adopt outsiders as family members rather quickly. Perhaps it has something to do with the manner in which the outsider is allowed to assume the same dominance over them as the parent(s). Perhaps it is not a compliment or term of endearment at all.

I called the detective at the Sheriff's department who took more interest in the story. Since I learned that Steve was not a relative, this was actually a case of child sexual assault, which should be reported to law enforcement instead of DSS. Two detectives immediately came to the school and interviewed the children before taking them to be tested and questioned further. The detectives, a male and a female, later told me that the two victims' stories were consistent, and that they had no doubt that each child told the truth. They informed me that there would probably be a warrant for Steve's arrest.

Several months later I learned that Uncle Steve had been arrested and charged with several counts of indecent liberties with minors, including rape.

Weeks afterwards, the local newspaper put his picture on the front page and an article below that explained that he received a sentence of over 40 years in prison. His bushy mustache and fat face characterized his mug shot, but I looked for something different in his eyes. I could see nothing, no sign that he was a predator. However, I could only imagine how venomous that face must have been to the children as he victimized them. The horror of the testimonies and the defense's cross-examinations must have compounded the shame and guilt. I am sure this entire ordeal was disappointing to Steve because he would never realize his dream; his application to operate a children's group home just three houses away from a school was being processed when Bus 355 came to screeching halt that winter morning because two children, standing in the cold, were beating on each other in an attempt to make sense of their similar fates.

Starla and David may have confronted Uncle Steve, but there is an abundance of painful healing that will have to be dealt with over the courses of their lives. They agreed to cooperate with law enforcement, see psychiatrists, and let me know if there is ever another problem I can help them resolve. They moved to the mountains, perhaps an evasive measure on the part of the parents to shed the accusations of neglect that led to the sexual assault. The children and parents escaped to form a new beginning, but are probably realizing that changing the scenery has little to do with healing. Although Steve was removed from their paths and his physical dominance will never threaten them again, he will continue to rape their emotions and haunt most every opportunity for happiness for years to follow. The last I heard, Steve was appealing his conviction.

DIRTY SOCKS

As an administrator I am witness to an unseen population of students falling victim to the various forms of abuse and neglect. There is no established method for teachers to recognize the symptoms of child abuse, with the exception of reporting the obvious exposed bruises. And there is no technique that is being taught to help the abused regain their balance and focus to overcome this adversity. Teachers need the power to hear their cries and the ability to feed their malnourished minds. Suspensions, inadequate federal programs, standardized testing, and various forms of competition create a current in the school that sweeps the abused children into corners. There are millions of Phillips out there, like tiny birds in a robin's nest, their wings have been healing when they should have been developing. They cannot support themselves when the others are nudged from the treetops to flutter to nearby perches. Instead, they spiral downward, out of control, and crash into the hardness and cruelty of the earth below. And we watch and shrug our shoulders, walking away, mumbling something that sounds a lot like, "No child left behind." The fact that most school districts give more staff development to help empower teachers with "test-taking techniques" than they do in recognizing and reporting child abuse is absurd. How can schools allow this to occur without acknowledging that such a high percentage of children come to them each day, broken, hungry, beaten, and ridiculed? It seems that the adults are so preoccupied with their mission statements they forget to properly prepare their missionaries. Educators must be concerned with the legalities surrounding the reporting of child abuse. In most cases teachers are informed that they have a *legal* obligation to report such incidents, but educators should feel a *moral* obligation to get involved. Child abuse is the 800-pound gorilla in the room nobody in education intelligently acknowledges. By perusing school board policies and teacher manuals, there is little mention of this tremendous threat to children and what teachers should look for or how they should respond, but there are detailed descriptions of what constitutes an illegal bandana or sagging pants. They go to great lengths to describe inappropriate body piercing, but when I asked a local board member what precautions are in place to assist and protect teachers in abuse assessment and reporting, he ended the conversation; frankly, he had no idea. Neither did the principal when confronted with the same question, even though his answer took three minutes. The bottom line: educational leaders consider it somebody else's job, leaving it to Child Protective Services (CPS) and law enforcement officials as often as possible. It is the mosquito of educational politics, unconsciously brushed away but always around and always a threat. A problem nobody feels should fall on his or her respective plate. CPS is not funded to handle the mere fraction of the problems that get reported. Federal and state governments are not prepared to treat this epidemic, so if they ignore the problem long enough, the cries of the children will be drowned out by the din of voices from countless others in need of services. With few adult advocates (parents and educators), the child cannot get the attention of those who can help. Many fall by the wayside, absorbed by the ills of society, to later pass their fates onto their own children.

Essentially, every other aspect of a child's well being is addressed. 504 plans are designed to give children an equal footing when disabilities threaten learning. Hearing and vision are tested and nurses administer necessary vaccines and monitor shot records. Emergency procedures outline steps to protect children from intruders, fires, and threatening weather. Dogs sniff school lockers to keep drugs out of our children's hands, while resource officers frisk suspects for knives and guns. Principals and school nurses rush emergencies to hospitals and provide insurance and expensive protective equipment for student athletes. Translators are hired for children who speak foreign languages. Breakfast and lunch are given to those who cannot afford to eat properly. Initiatives to improve relations with parents dodge this delicate issue. If communications are in tact that announce bad weather or athletic contests, why is the same system not in place for reporting domestic violence perpetrated against our children? Yet somehow, something that kills a large number of children annually, something that causes various forms of mental retardation, destroys any hope of a normal adulthood, wrecks lives, sabotages marriages, and populates our prisons, is not the responsibility of public education. School is the one institution that can protect, nurture, and mend child abuse, but its power is wasted in a bureaucratic slumber. In fact, some school systems today still endorse the use of corporal punishment, which illustrates how blind they are to this tragic problem.

According to an article in *Education Digest* that questions why school health officials remain largely silent on child abuse and neglect, there are no valid reasons why we have excluded child abuse and neglect treatment from our curricula.[3] It adds that a review by the National Research Council of the National Academy of Sciences indicates, "85% of child abuse and neglect deaths have been 'systematically misidentified.'"[4] In other words, there is no urgency because the problem is being buried by the government services that, as mentioned, are under-funded and overworked. Misdiagnoses skew data that reflects the enormity of the problem. A report from the U.S. Advisory Board on Child Abuse and Neglect says, "The misery caused by near-fatal abuse and neglect ripples through this country, each year leaving 18,000 permanently disabled children . . . tens of thousands of victims overwhelmed by lifelong psychological trauma . . . who, as adults, continue to bear the psychological scars."[5]

Recently a father came to see me because his son, a Latino who is one of the most humble and kind students in the sixth grade, was having trouble catching the bus. He explained that Alex had difficulty reporting his problem because he functions on the level of a six-year-old. The discussion led to the father's allegation that Alex recently had money taken from him on the bus, but neither he nor Alex could provide names or details. The father suddenly became angry by my reaction or lack of one, and stood and leaned on my desk. "If you don't find out who took that $5.00 from Alex, I will. When I find out, they will wish you had gotten to them first."

"Mr. Torres, you will not be investigating, confronting, or threatening any student in this school. I was willing to look into this, but right now it seems you are the biggest concern I need to deal with. Unless you want to get arrested, I suggest that you change your approach."

"You don't scare me. I have been in prison before and I would go again in a minute for my son!"

"Would you go back to prison over five bucks?" I should have just asked him to leave and saved the sarcasm for another day, but I am not good at that. Whatever disorder Mr. Torres has I probably have as well, which made our conversation pointless.

He became very angry. His arms flinched, which drew my attention to the homemade tattoos on his hands. The row of indistinguishable blue letters across his knuckles didn't surprise me. Every time I had seen that in the past, it had been the markings of a gang member or inmate. It was my guess that he wanted me to see them to intimidate me, but I am not from his world, so they did not. Besides, I didn't see his gang in the office, and I have never feared ink on skin. I did fear for Alex, however. Before I enraged him any further with my stinging sarcasm and ever so pungent wit, I stood and asked him to leave. He obliged, but not without the stare that was intended to frighten me, but I was too busy to give it a lot of thought.

I notified every adult in the building that I was concerned for Alex's safety. I asked his E.C. teacher to look for specific signs and report them to me if she found any. On the following Monday after his father's visit, that same teacher received a phone call from a local elementary school, where Alex's stepbrother and sister attend. They had noticed some unmistakable belt marks inside the arm of Alex's sister, and wanted to alert other schools that also may have a child in danger. I admire the school for their observant and proactive approach to the issue. Their concern for all children who might be involved, regardless of the school that child may attend, sports the philanthropic spirit that all schools need to combat this problem. Mrs. Funderburk had Alex waiting outside my office door by the time I knew about the problem. He also had visible bruises. A brief conversation with him revealed the horror of his weekend. His slurred speech, hunger for positive attention, stunted cognitive development, difficulty processing questions and formulating responses suggested to me that his abuse had been going on a long time, perhaps since shortly after he was born. I suspect that abuse is why he is in the exceptional children's program. His brain development was likely stunted by extreme, persistent trauma and excessive physical brutality.

He had bruises from various beatings. The bluish marks on his legs were faded and, according to Alex's best estimation, about a week old. He pulled down his pants (without being asked to) and showed marks that were more recent. They had a purple quality and distinctive lines that revealed the width of the belt. He then told me a story that occurred the day before. It took a while because his slurred speech and limited intelligence slowed the process considerably, but Alex was sincere, perhaps not able to mentally process a lie. Mrs. Funderburk and I sat motionless through every desperate word.

Alex's stepmother asked him to go outside and take off his dirty socks. He didn't do it, later explaining that he was watching television and didn't hear her. His father flew in from the other room because the stepmother had to tell him again. With his tattooed fists, he punched Alex, "four or five or three times" in the side of his head while he sat defenseless. He didn't get out of the chair as directed; his father and stepmother were yelling at him while he covered his head crying. Dad lifted the chair into the air and dumped Alex onto the floor, where he kicked him. Since we had heard enough, Mrs. Funderburk and I called CPS and reported the abuse.

That Wednesday Alex told his teacher that "the government" was at his house. I was relieved, but then he refused to answer my casual questions, telling Mrs. Funderburk and me that his father told him that he is never to talk to us about him again. CPS sent a form letter to follow up on my report, which basically stated that Alex's dad was being investigated and that they would be in contact if I would be needed any further. "Neglect" was the basis for the interventions. Neglect?

My experience has been that many parents who abuse children are very familiar with CPS and do not seem to fear their periodic investigations. These parents know the game and how to bend the rules. I suppose we should feel fortunate that Alex's father was investigated when forty-eight percent of his home state's reported cases are not. In fact, we identified the problem for them with documentation and witnesses. Frankly, even with the considerable evidence we gave them, one would wonder how the child could remain in the house. We hoped for the best. However, as adults we must not confuse governmental intervention with justice. We need not assume all federal and state programs are functional, funded properly, and sufficiently staffed. I didn't feel as if I assisted Alex; I felt that I passed him along. Again, I had no choice.

It is frustrating to have been physically and verbally abused as a child, even more frustrating when I consider the actuality that my childhood was abnormal and at the core of nearly every adult problem I have, but nothing compares to the emptiness I felt when the only bullet I had in my chamber to protect this child misfired. Mrs. Funderburk became upset, fearing that the perceived incompetence of the CPS officer would only make Alex's father more brash and arrogant. She was correct.

Until things change, educators are very limited in their abilities to figuratively raid the home with the available resources to save children. They can, however, help children that they strongly suspect are abused and give them an antidote to the poison they get at home. The job of the educator is to protect and educate the child. We also need to give him or her the security, confidence, and equal opportunity to succeed. The most important thing we can do is to provide an environment where everybody is nurtured and supported. According to Ron Edmonds, "A school can create a coherent environment so potent that for at least six hours a day it can override almost everything else in the lives of children."[6] But somehow, the modern school has lost its way. Schools are now microcosms of the industrialized, competitive, "dog-eat-dog" world, where children are systematically measured against one another and then classified and labeled by adults. We create winners and losers, passers and failures, and leaders and followers. Some are praised and promoted in life, and others are rejected with all the warmth that Charles Darwin's mother must have shown him.

NOTES

1. *The Lion King*, Walt Disney Pictures, 1994.
2. Phillip Ney ,Tak Fung, and Adele Wickett, "The Worst Combinations of Child Abuse and Neglect," *Child Abuse and Neglect,* 18, no.9, (1994): 705–714.
3. William Sechrist, "Why Teach About Child Abuse and Neglect?" *Education Digest,* 66 no.2, (2000): 45.
4. Sechrist, "Why Teach," 45.
5. Sechrist, "Why Teach," 45.
6. Ron Edmonds, "School Violence Prevention: Protective Processes Within Schools," *U.S. Department of Health and Human Services.* <http://www. mentalhealth .org/schoolviolence/part1chp14.asp> (27 Dec. 2005).

Chapter Three

Defense Mode

"We know what we are, but know not what we may be."

—William Shakespeare, *Hamlet*

STRESS FRACTURES

Albert Camus once said, "Perhaps we cannot prevent this world from being a world in which children are tortured, but we can reduce the number of tortured children . . . I continue to struggle against a universe in which children suffer and die."[1] Child abuse devastates the growth of a small, helpless individual on such a large scale it is nearly impossible to have a fruitful and productive life without some sort of intervention and salvation during the developmental years. We live in an era when our government leaders have decided to overhaul education by a doctrine of accountability that is packaged with the nifty slogans and rhetorical objectives. The creation of numbers, basically, measured in no more than four-year cycles and twisted to praise the incumbents and manipulated to defeat them by political adversaries. However, the data that is available to school administrators and politicians suggest that educational leaders and well-intending politicians have omitted a rather significant subgroup that will undoubtedly lead to the failure of any reformative movement because it leaves children hidden in secrecy and behind labels.

Perhaps the first American study of the effects of child abuse and neglect is the most telling. The H. M. Skeels study (1937) states:

> The beneficial effect on intellectual growth of transferring neglected, abused, and homeless infants from custodial placement in the sterile environment of a

> state institution for mental defectives of similar age to the corresponding institution where, administratively, they were the guests of the inmates, who lavished on them much care and attention. The state administrative bureaucracy soon put a stop to this iconoclastic guest program, thus inadvertently providing a contrast group of children, not originally retarded mentally, who became retarded in the sterile environment of a custodial institution for the irrevocably brain damaged and retarded.[2]

Thirty years later, a determined Skeels (1966) conducted a follow-up study on the participants, then adults, obviously. He found that the infants who received the motherly fondling, interaction and emotional stimulation had been adopted at a much higher rate, succeeded in school, held down responsible jobs and provided for their families. The others had done poorly in special education classes for the learning disabled, in vocational programs, and had difficulty securing regular employment. They did not establish family households and, if they had children, did not support them. Their I.Q. scores were permanently defective, while their counterparts had average I.Q. scores.[3]

Phillip was a learning-disabled student in a self-contained program. The two adults who had the opportunity to interact with him regularly were his teacher, Mrs.Cryer, and Mrs. Gamble, a sixty-year-old teacher assistant. Between the two, they had received absolutely no training in the recognition of the symptoms of child abuse, although both had been in education for nearly 50 years. Nonetheless, it is possible that some in the exceptional children's program are labeled as such because their abuse caused a deficiency in learning abilities. Phillip's lack of cognitive development, family dynamics, father's drug and drinking problem, and other factors made him one of the most probable candidates for persistent child abuse. However, he went unnoticed through the school system for over six years, with the exception of his constant behavior problems and inability to learn basic educational functions, until he walked into my office. Since educators are not trained in recognizing abuse but have become experts in the administration of labels, it probably took a formerly-abused, grown child to spot one.

American social and developmental psychologist Wayne Dennis conducted a study unrelated to that of Skeels but complimentary in findings. His subjects were Lebanese children who were suddenly made available for adoption after a 1956 law change. The older group, which had been wards of the institution all of their lives and had been exposed to harsh and abusive conditions, had an average I.Q. score of 50, while the younger children who were adopted by age two averaged a score of 100. His study concluded that a child living in abusive and neglectful conditions loses up to six months of intellectual development every year.[4] This suggests that abuse and emotional neglect alone cause the child to cognitively develop at a much slower rate than that of other children. If this included educational neglect and the failure to provide basic needs like food, shelter, and hygiene, one could hypothesize that the rate of development might exceed 50 percent of their well-adjusted peers. Over the period of several years, the difference is astounding, which explains the likelihood that these children would be placed in exceptional children's classes (Alex's father explained to me that his son, age 12, functioned on the level of a six-year-old). Skeels' study basically addresses the problem of neglect that begins early in childhood without involving abuse, and, while Dennis takes a look at neglect and abuse, his findings exclude social, emotional, and physical development. Due to laws protecting the rights and confidentiality of subjects in studies of this nature, and because parental consent is required, it is difficult to find contemporary studies that link abuse and cognitive development. However, in more recent studies that perhaps were spawned from these pioneering efforts, there are clear links between neglect/abuse and later psychological, emotional, behavioral and social disorders.

During the last twenty-five years much more has been learned about child abuse than ever before. Aside from physical impairments and injuries caused by abuse and neglect, the emotional and cognitive prices are steeper than one ever imagined. According to the *American Academy of Child Adolescent Psychiatry*, it was learned that children who experience extreme or chronic stressors suffer from post-traumatic stress disorder (PTSD), the same affliction associated with Vietnam veterans.[5] However, an opinion that the effects are identical is erroneous. New research since the early 1980s has determined that child abuse and neglect during infancy and early childhood actually hinder brain development, which supports the findings of Dennis and Skeels. "It is now clear that what a child experiences in the first few years of his life largely determines how his brain will develop and how he will interact with the world throughout his life."[6] The stress that humans experience is the body's way to survive environmental pressures and threats. Much has been researched about the effects of stress in adults, but the levels of stress that occur in children who are exposed to long-term and chronic abuse and neglect are more problematic. Basically, the child stays in survival mode and many parts of his brain are not developed. According to Dr. Bruce D. Perry, creator of *Child-Trauma.org.,* the following situation occurs:

> Chronic stress or repeated traumas can result in a number of biological reactions. Neurochemical systems are affected which can cause a cascade of changes in attention, impulse control, sleep, and fine motor control. . . . Chronic activation of certain parts of the brain involved in the fear response . . . can "wear out" other parts of the brain such as the hippocampus, which is involved in cognition and memory.[7]

Not only are memory and learning affected, there are other physical deficiencies created when the brain stays on the defense mode. "Early experiences of trauma can also interfere with the development of the subcortical and limbic systems which can result in extreme anxiety, depression, and difficulty forming attachments to other people."[8] In essence, the stress associated with abuse is damaging both cognitively and socially. While the brain's defense mechanism may be necessary to survive in a hostile world, experts agree that the long-term effects are difficult to reverse, creating a child or adult who is reactive, secluded, depressed, and unpredictable. This is what caused PTSD in soldiers who had year-long tours of duty. However, the adult brain is fully developed, so the imbalance seems to be more social than developmental. With children, the tour of duty is much longer, and the impact is arguably more devastating and less treatable because it interferes with normal brain development.

PTSD is undoubtedly more frequently associated with the soldiers returning from the Vietnam War than with young children, when over three million men saw active combat over a 12-year period. Over the next 20 years, a full 30 percent developed PTSD.[9] According to The Child Trauma Academy, "In 1995, nearly 3 million children were exposed to traumatic abuse and neglect in the United States, a 42% increase from a decade earlier."[10] In 1995 alone, the number of children exposed to the trauma of abuse is identical to the total number of Americans who served our country in combat during the entire American involvement in Vietnam.[11] It also suggests that it is a conservative assumption to estimate that the trauma children experience is similar; the more accurate assumption is that it is more devastating. Of those 12 million soldiers, nearly one third developed PTSD.[12] If the current trend continues, it is possible that as many as 12 million children annually will develop cognitive and psychological problems (such as PTSD) related to traumatic abuse and neglect.[13] It remains to be determined exactly how much more dramatic and damaging traumatic stress must be on children exposed to chronic violence or abuse during their most vulnerable years, during the time they are developing socially, cognitively, physically, and emotionally. There is very limited support for specific treatments. According to the *Journal of the American Academy of Child and Adolescent Psychiatry*, the process used for treating adults, cognitive behavior treatment (CBT), is considered to be the best available treatment for children.[14]

Yet young brains are much more susceptible to PTSD because they are developing and defining their environments at a much more rapid pace than adults. According to the *PTSD Alliance*, victims of childhood abuse who are at a tremendous risk for PTSD may be difficult to detect because symptoms might not occur immediately after the trauma.[15] There is a vast array of characteristics that might be otherwise difficult to diagnose. Soldiers who experience PTSD are more readily treatable because the source of the disorder is easily identifiable.

In an attempt to generalize a rather complex analysis and description of the brain's component areas and their primary functions, it is essential for the various regions to be joined by a series of synaptic connections. A fully integrated brain requires connections between the hemispheres by the corpus callosum. Psychologist Arthur Becker-Weidman of the Center for Family Development details the reasons the brains of abused and neglected children are underdeveloped:

> Abused and neglected children have a smaller corpus collosum than non-abused children. Abused and neglected children have poorly integrated cerebral hemispheres. This poor integration of hemispheres is and underdevelopment of the orbitofrontal cortex is the basis for such symptoms as difficulty regulating emotion, lack of cause-effect thinking, inability to accurately recognize emotions in others, inability of the child to articulate the child's own emotions, and incoherent sense of self and autobiographical history, and a lack of conscious.[16]

Because the brains of abused children are not as well integrated as those of non-abused children, abused children have difficulties emotional regulation, cognition or processing, and social development.[17] In fact, brains of maltreated children can be 20 to 30 percent smaller than those of non-maltreated children.[18]

It is interesting that the orbitofrontal cortex, which houses conscience development and the capacity for empathy, is also sensitive to face recognition and eye contact. Perhaps an inability in one of these areas, as was the case with Phillip's prolonged blank gazes at my rather uneventful stapler to avoid my piercing stare, was a clue that could have led me to more of an understanding that the abuse had been over a longer period of time than I imagined. That would have been useful if having to determine if Maw Maw, who recently joined the Gregg clan, or Dad were responsible for the abuse.

According to Wayne Kritsberg , a therapist who specializes in dealing with adults who were abused children, the functional family is very different from the dysfunctional (abusive or neglecting) family. In *The Adult Children of Alcoholics Syndrome*, resiliency is the child's ability to overcome trauma or a setback, which is referred to as "shock." When the dysfunctional family does not assist in the rebound and resolution stages that follow shock, then the child goes into a shutdown mode. "He is unable to talk about his emotions to anyone in the family. . . . The child has no one to turn to, and no one who is safe enough for him to express those feelings that are bottled up."[19]

As an adult, I have developed amnesia about many events of my childhood, which is a coping technique that I unknowingly utilized to help establish resiliency. As a child, however, I had stomach problems that caused nausea and occasionally would actually vomit anticipating an abusive situation, even if I was not the target. Research reveals that different age groups respond differently to stressors that trigger PTSD.[20] When the stomachaches faded away just before puberty, I developed intense migraine headaches that would prohibit any exposure to light or physical movement for at least twenty-four hours. My parents took me to the hospital for X-rays and a brain scan to grasp the reason for this sudden outbreak; the doctor explained that there seemed to be a "slight abnormality" in my brain, one that I could overcome as I continued to develop. My parents dismissed it as something minor, and I had to endure jokes about it for a good while. It is interesting to note that when I left home for college, the migraines stopped within a few months. I continued to get a few pre-migraine symptoms when stressed, like a partial loss of vision and nausea, but the migraines themselves faded away.

Stress brought on by the memory of the abuse can occur for years after the traumatic event or series of events. Time does not heal these wounds as with other injuries. Often, childhood scars are carried deep into adulthood. A person cannot internalize the trauma because it continues to haunt the victim until it is rejected by the mind at an emotional cost. There is no way anyone can understand Starla and David without first comprehending the world in which they live. The fists they were throwing at the bus stop and the insults they shouted were their way of releasing the stress associated with abuse. When they described how Uncle Steve threatened them if they ever told anyone, how he abused them under the guise of punishment so they would feel the shame and guilt of the trauma, I understood how much courage it took to tell me. According to *The Royal College of Psychiatrists*, children can be secretive about the abuse because they may have been threatened or feel the abuse is their fault, like Starla and David.[21]

The problem for educators is found in detection and the responsibilities, both legal and ethical, which coincide with an act as bold as reporting suspected abuse. Unless there is physical evidence, it is difficult for an educator to detect abuse. Teachers are not psychologists and so much of the abuse, including the physical, is psychological. As early as third grade, teachers might be responsible for over 125 students each day. It would be detrimental in the establishment of rapport with the parents and community if teachers have every possible abusive family investigated. They may also know or love the abuser and want to protect her or him. They might feel that reporting the offense would break up the family, causing them to be separated from other family members they love.[22]

Abused and neglected children are difficult to identify because their behaviors vary depending on the type and length of the abuse. "Children are often characterized by developmental delays, fear of strangers, trouble socializing with peers, disruptive behavior, and poor school performance."[23] Adolescents turn their rage inward. Their behavior features delinquencies, eating disorders, truancy, self-mutilation, and suicide. Alert and trained teachers who know the subtle signs of the abused child can monitor interpersonal friction in classrooms. Abused children are insecure with their parents or caregivers, have few close friends, have difficulty trusting others, and display a fear of intimacy.[24]

More difficult to detect is an abused child's self-perception. They usually suffer from extremely low self-esteem to such a degree that it often coincides with severe depression. All abuse is emotional, which makes it difficult to detect at times because children have difficulty expressing themselves, especially under extremely stressful circumstances. Psychological maltreatment consists of the following:

> (1) discipline and control techniques which are based on fear and intimidation, (2) low quantity of human interaction in which (caregivers) communicate a lack of interest, caring and affection, (3) limited opportunities for (children) to develop adequate skills or feelings of self-worth, (4) encouragement to be dependent and subservient, and (5) denial of opportunities for healthy risk-taking.[25]

Not only are these characteristics applicable to abusive parents, they are also applicable to teachers who demand obedience, disseminate knowledge, and disregard the importance of the student-teacher relationship. Imagine the impact on a child exposed to both on a daily basis.

These consequences obviously take their toll on the child whose goals are not to succeed, but to survive in a world where normal is a foreign concept. Parents are not a source of stability but the reason for a child's inability to trust others and love himself.

Friends are often threats to the intimate secrets that haunt the abused and neglected child. There are no human vessels for sharing, only judges and enemies. Considering the chaos that characterizes life at home, there is no haven where the child feels safe from the world. Nor is there a mindset where the child feels safe to experience the world, unless the child finds the strength to trust a potential enemy and confide in an adult. For many, school is the last resort. According to data accumulated in 1997 by the *National Foundation for Abused and Neglected Children* from forty-four responding states, 90 percent of the perpetrators of child maltreatment (a combination of abuse and assault) were parents and or relatives.[26] This suggests that the only way protective agencies might be alerted to the abuse or neglect of a child is by identifying marks of physical abuse or by the admission of the victim. Considering that the child's caretakers might be the only other adults regularly in the company of the child, educators have a tremendous responsibility, one that they are not prepared to handle, according to the statistics. "Although the majority of the abused children in the United States are of school age, school staffs are responsible for only about 15 percent of cases reported each year."[27] Take into account that there is evidence to suggest that the number of abused children reported to CPS could be lower than an estimated thirty percent of all cases of child abuse, then the significance of educators in the battle against child abuse is alarmingly miniscule, especially after considering that educators are with students for about 1,200 hours per year. Because child abuse by its nature is allusive, statistics that estimate how widespread the problem is have become varied. The truth is that child abuse is a hidden problem that we cannot easily measure. However, even if these minimal percentages are exclusively examined, the range still covers too high a percentage of children to ignore. They also reveal some rather disturbing trends that are directly associated with poverty and parental support. This by no means suggests that any race, socio-economic status, or family framework is immune.

In a more recent study than the previously referenced, Nancy Rayome of Cornell University determined that although poverty, socioeconomic background, and family structure are distinguishing variables, child abuse is constantly and consistently linked to academic failure. She concludes, "maltreatment is an additional factor over and above poverty that impacts on the academic skills of these children."[28] Nonetheless, the statistics are overwhelming. For example, in the congressionally-mandated *Third National Incidence Study on Child Abuse and Neglect* data that reflects some interesting trends in the composition of the American family seem to conflict with recent educational reform:

> First, one must question the dedication to address the needs of children who live in poverty. NIS-3 reveals that the number of abused and neglected children almost doubled from 1986 to1993, when the total number of children seriously injured and endangered quadrupled. Alarmingly, the report also concluded that children who live in poverty are 22 times more likely to be abused or neglected, 56 times more likely to be educationally neglected, 18 times more likely to be sexually molested, and 60 times more likely to die from abusive injuries than children in families whose income exceeds $30,000 per year.[29]

The report added that children who live in single-parent homes have a 220 percent greater risk of being educationally neglected than children with married parents living at home. These statistics were presented to Congress *before* the "No Child Left Behind" (NCLB) program was being processed into law. With information from NIC-3 in hand, it would seem that things might also be done to target the life-long problems surrounding child abuse and recognize the detrimental impact it is certain to have on NCLB.

It is logical to implement programs to help educators recognize and address the issues surrounding this epidemic that threatens our children, loads exceptional children's classes, creates unemployment, fills prisons, and is passed from generation to generation like a sacred family heirloom. But there was more legislation in the early stages of the George W. Bush administration that sent a different signal to our desperate children. According to *Children's Defense Fund* of 2002, the $1.6 trillion tax cut Bush proposed aided the wealthy, the top one percent of the incomes in the nation, more than it assisted the bottom 20 percent.[30] This budget cut the Child Abuse Discretionary Fund nearly 46 percent, from $33 million to under $18 million. The proposal also froze or cut other discretionary funds for children in 14 areas, totaling a $3.1 billion reduction.[31] The tax breaks that provided for the top one percent in America were put into perspective by providing the following list of interventions that the United States could implement with the money it cost to provide the tax cut:

> 1) Provide health insurance for every uninsured child in America (approximately 11 percent are uninsured), 2) Provide Head Start preschool and quality child care for every eligible child in need, 3) Provide housing vouchers for the parents of the 3.6 million children whose parents pay more than half of their income on rent or live in subsidized housing, 4) Provide services to protect millions of abused and neglected children.[32]

School employees are instructed to report all suspected cases of child abuse to CPS, but available resources do not always protect the child. It seems that some are token programs designed to combat growing problems with decreasing budgets. This why Phillip, an illiterate middle school student, knew that his problems would only get "worser" if I helped. In a letter featured on the National Association of Social Worker's web site, the problem of under funding was addressed:

> The nation's child welfare system has long been stretched beyond capacity to handle the full scope of child maltreatment. While report after report has been issued about a system sorely in need of resources, funds for CAPTA programs have been nearly frozen for a decade. Far too little attention is directed at preventing harm to children from happening in the first place or providing the

> appropriate services and treatment needed by families and children victimized by abuse or neglect. . . Nationally, average caseloads for child welfare workers are double the recommended caseload. . . . Billions of dollars are spent every year on foster care—too often the only option for families in crisis. Very little money is spent on the front-end, prevention programs. If we could invest in proven prevention programs and strategies designed at the local level to meet individual family and community needs, we could reduce the expenditure for costly back-end crisis services.[33]

A combination of high caseloads, worker turnover, and low salaries critically impedes the delivery of services at the expense of our children. According to the *Child Welfare League of America in North Carolina*, the minimum salary for a caseworker responsible for investigating reports was $15,000 per year in 2000.[34] According to North Carolina CPS's data from 2001–02, only 52 percent of the reported cases were ever investigated. Scotland County's CPS department investigated only seven percent of all reported cases. Six other counties investigated fewer than 20 percent.[35] Once the child slips through the school and CPS's porous screen, there is little anyone can do until the victim initiates the action. For some, the next step is incarceration, as was the case with my brother, uncles, and countless others.

CAGED BIRDS

About a third of all women in American prisons reported abuses as children, which is nearly three times the entire female population's estimated 12 to 17 percent. About 14 percent of the male inmates reported abuse as children, with the estimates of the normal population ranging from five to eight percent.[36] Aside from the fact that these statistics indicate that child abuse (note that these statistics do not include neglect) is eventually contributing to the prison population, it is noteworthy to take into account the percentages of the general population who reported being abused. Combining these percentages suggests that the abused population of American citizens falls somewhere between eight and nearly 13 percent of the general population. According to this data, educators should assume that one of every ten students is being abused. This contradicts data from the department of social services, but their data is so skewed because it relies on the cases actually being reported and then being accepted by the agency.

In a recent study in Alaskan prisons involving long-term inmates, the figures are even higher. A shocking 80 percent of the inmates surveyed described some form of physical abuse in their childhoods, while over 70 percent experienced some type of sexual abuse.[37] According to The Alaska Justice Statistical Analysis Center, 100 percent (52 of 52) of the long-term inmates surveyed who were convicted of at least three juvenile crimes, suffered from child abuse and neglect.[38] The study was conducted to examine a cycle of violence to see if and how abuse correlates with harmful aggression. These staggering statistics suggest that it might be more cost effective to increase spending in the area of child abuse instead of cutting funding for children's discretionary funds. For example, recent research presents the case for additional government intervention in terms of "Rates of Return to Human Capital Investment:"

> Citing a 1993 study of 123 young African-American children he finds early intervention ultimately contributes to greater tax revenue and also identifies possible cost savings in the areas justice, mental health and welfare. The study concludes that every dollar invested in Child Protective Services produces a return of $7.16.[39]

It would seem that the wise strategy might be to address the issues that seem to harbor a high percentage of child abuse that is, essentially, the result of society's frustration.

Of course, this is not to suggest that all abused children end up on death row. Miraculously, many survive the ordeal without major, noticeable setbacks. In fact, there are many success stories. There are stories of people who extricate themselves from these horrible circumstances to assume positions of great power and responsibility. Alice Miller, in her book entitled *For Your Own Good,* describes the abuse of a young Austrian boy who rose to an adulthood of fame and great accomplishments. The boy had a father who, as a youth, was beaten with a whip by his stepfather, who in turn, beat the young boy to the point where he recalled his sisters eagerly trying to pull his enraged father off him. The boy remembered "growing up with his parent and four siblings in two basement rooms, watching his father beat his mother and seeing 'things that can fill even an adult with nothing but horror.'"[40] At the age of 11, he was nearly beaten to death for trying to run away. His older brother, 14, was more successful, leaving home never to see his father again. "Later, the only thing he would remember with pride from that childhood was being able to deaden himself so thoroughly that he could take thirty two whiplashes from his father without making a sound."[41]

I realized that he had discovered a secret that I too had learned; we both seemed to have formed mental, protective bowers where we were immune to pain. And like me, he would survive his childhood abuse and reach far beyond his own or anyone else's expectations. I would become an educational leader who earned a doctorate degree and became a college professor. That Austrian boy would also learn to adapt and succeed. He would move to Germany, determined to avenge the horrors of his childhood, arguably achieving more power and reputation than any other man in the modern world. And like me, Adolph Hitler somehow avoided prison. One never knows how beneficial it is to society to save a child from abuse, or how costly an abused child can become.

NOTES

1. Albert Camus, "Quotes on Young People," *The Freechild Project* 1948, <http://www.freechild.org/quotations.htm> (May 20, 2006).

2. John Money, "Child Abuse: Growth Failure, IQ Deficit, and Learning," *Journal of Learning Disabilities* 15, no. 10 (1982).

3. Money, "Child Abuse."

4. Wayne Dennis, *Children of the Creche*, (New York: Appleton-Century Crofts, 1973).

5. Judith Cohen, "Practice Parameters for the Assessment and Treatment of Children and Adolescents with Posttraumatic Stress Disorder," *American Academy of Child Adolescent Psychiatry* 37, no. 9 (October, 1998): 997–1001.

6. Rima Shore, *Rethinking the Brain.* (New York: Families and Work Institute, 1997): 40.

7. Bruce Perry, "Traumatized Children: How Childhood Trauma Influences Brain Development," *Baylor College of Medicine* 2000, <http://www.bcm.tmc.edu/cta/trau_CAMI.htm> (22 Feb. 2005).

8. Shore, *Rethinking the Brain*, 40.

9. Bruce Perry, "Neurodevelopment and the Neurophysiology of Trauma I: Conceptual Considerations for Clinical Work with Maltreated Children. *APSAC Advisor* 6, no. 1, (1993): 1–18.

10. Bruce Perry, David Conrad, Christine Dobson, Stephanie Schick, and Duane Runyan, "The Children's Crisis Care Center Model," *Child Trauma Academy, Department of Psychiatry and Behavioral Medicine, Baylor College of Medicine* 2004, <www.ChildTrauma.org> (1 March 2006).

11. Bruce Perry, "Neurobiological Sequelae of Childhood Trauma: Post-traumatic Stress in Children," *Catecholamines in Post-traumatic Stress Disorder Emerging Concepts*, (Washington, D.C.: American Psychiatric Press, 2004): 253–276.

12. Perry, "Neurobiological Sequelae," 255.

13. Perry, "Neurobiological Sequelae," 255.

14. Jessica Hamblen, "PTSD in Children and Adolescents," *National Center for Post Traumatic Stress Disorder, U.S. Department of Veteran Affairs* 2007, <http://www.ncptsd.va.gov/ncmain/ncdocs/fact_shts/fs_children.html> (3 June 2007).

15. "Myths about Posttraumatic Stress Disorder," *PTSD Alliance* 2006, <http://www.ptsdalliance.org> (5 March 2006).

16. ArthurBecker-Weidman, *Child Abuse and Neglect* 2006, <http://www.mental-health-matters.com/articles/article.php?artID=581> (8 March 2006).

17. Julia Neuberger, "Brain Development Research: Wonderful Window of Opportunity to Build Public Support for Childhood Education," *Young Children* 52, no.1, (1997): 4–9.

18. Barbara Lowenthal, "The Effects of Maltreatment and Ways to Promote Children's Resiliency," *Childhood Education* 75, no. 4 (1999): 204–09.

19. Wayne Kritsberg, *The Adult Children of Alcoholics Syndrome*, (New York: Bantam, 1985): 56.

20. "Myths about Posttraumatic Stress Disorder," Hamblin, "PTSD"

21. "Child Abuse and Neglect: The Emotional Effects," *The Royal College of Psychiatrists,* 2005, <http://www.rcpsych.ac.uk.info/mhgu/newmhgu19.htm> (1 March 2005).

22. "Child Abuse and Neglect: The Emotional Effects."

23. Douglas Barnett, Jody Todd Manly, and Dante Cicchetti, "Defining Child Maltreatment: The Interface Between Policy and Research," in *Child Abuse, Child Development and Social Policy,* ed. D. Cicchetti & S. L. Toth, (Norwood, NJ: Ablex Publishing, 1993): 7–74.

24. Barnett, Manly, and Cicchetti, "Defining Child Maltreatment, 7–74.

25. Irwin Hyman, "The Enemy Within: Tales of Punishment, Politics, and Prevention," (paper presented at the Annual National Convention of School Psychologists, Atlanta, GA., March 1996).

26. "What is Child Abuse and Neglect?" *National Foundation for Abused and Neglected Children,* 1997, <http://www.gangfreekids.org> (15 March, 2004).

27. "Helping Abused Children," *Neshaminy (Pa) School District*, 2003, <http: //www .neshaminy.k12.pa.us> (10 Aug. 2005).

28. Nancy Reyome, "A Comparison of the School Performance of Sexually Abused, Neglected, and Non-maltreated Children," *Child Study Journal,* 23, no. 1 (1993): 17–39.

29. Andrea Sedlak and Diana Broadhurst, "Executive Summary of the Third National Incidence Study of Child Abuse and Neglect," *U.S. Department of Health and Human Services: Administration for Children and Families,* 1996, http://www.acf.org (5 March 2006).

30. "Child Abuse Statistics," *Children's Defense Fund,* 2002, <http://www. child defense.org> (11 Dec. 2003).

31. "Child Abuse Statistics."

32. "Child Abuse Statistics."

33. G. Miller and J.Greenwood, "Letter in Support of Child Welfare Funding," *National Association of Social Workers,* 2004, <http://www.naswc.org> (22 Sept. 2005).

34. "State Child Welfare Agency Survey," *National Data Analysis System*, 2001, <http://www.ndas.cwla.org/Report.asp?PageMode=&Report> (11 May 2004).

35. "Data and Statistics," *Action for Children: North Carolina,* 2002, <http:// www .ncchild.org/content/view/274/158/> (2 February 2003).

36. "National Child Abuse Statistics," *Childhelp USA*, 2005, <http://www.child-help usa.org> (5 March 2006).

37. "Inmate Histories: Evidence of Child Abuse," *Alaska Justice Forum*, 15, no. 3, 1998, <http://justice.uaa.alaska.edu/forum /f153fa98/a_inmante.html> (8 March 2005).
38. "Inmate Histories: Evidence of Child Abuse."
39. Ted Melhuish, "Child Protective Services," *Wikipedia*, 2007. <http://en.wikipedia.org/wiki/Child_protective_services#In_the_public_eye> (3 June 2007).
40. Gloria Steinem, *Revolution From Within,* (Boston: Little, Brown, 1992): 75.
41. Steinem, 75.

Chapter Four

The Sting of Competition

"Are we actually asked to love our neighbors and students? All of them? How is a teacher to love a child who does not achieve? What is the relationship between unconditional love and a hierarchical society?"

—David Purpel, *Moral Outrage in Education*

ORANGE PAPER

In May of 2005, I attended my son's fifth grade awards ceremony, located in the media center at his new, state-of-the-art school. The parents filed into the observation location where unfolded, metal chairs were carefully aligned to define the designated viewing area. The guests seemed confused and ignorant, like they had stepped out of time capsules into a fictional and distant future. I tuned in to individuals in the crowd who seemed peculiarly out of place. Some rambled on without purpose or point, like the elderly man offering epistles to everyone within an earshot, droning about the differences between this particular media center and the libraries of the mid-twentieth century. It seems whenever people congregate, there is always one who finds it necessary to talk very loudly to someone sitting right beside him, obviously intending for everyone around to hear. The rather undistinguished grandfather commented, "When I wuz in school we didn't even know what no computer wuz. They w' not no carpeted library and all da' books could fit on two a dem shelves." I waited for him to add, "And I turn't out just fine," but he stopped short of that, perhaps as if he figured that assumption was widely understood. The media center was impressive, having absorbed much of the funding that went into the $11 million facility that opened two years earlier. Since I was employed as an assistant principal who worked in a brand new middle school across the county, I could only imagine how such a room might amaze those in the crowd, aliens to contemporary education, some of whom last graced the halls of public schools when gas was a quarter. Their eyes pressed against every corner of the center, scanning it with a sense of unnecessary urgency, as they shared their exaggerated and nostalgic experiences. So there we sat, shoulder to shoulder with displaced strangers in this modern edifice, waiting for our little elementary school descendents to march in like robotic toy soldiers to have us praise, honor, and decorate them for rather routine and ordinary accomplishments.

My son Taylor has always been an excellent student, so, I must admit, I was inherently hoping he'd walk away with an armful of trophies, certificates, and ribbons. I imagined the moment when he approached the crowd at the end of the ceremony to hand me part of his load as we were leaving because his tender arms could not bear the burden of so many tokens of lofty adoration, justly signifying his academic supremacy and exemplary citizenship. Every one of those bumbling time-travelers would know that the little boy beneath the mound of accolades was my son. I would hear them whisper jealously to each other and congratulate Taylor with their smug, counterfeit clichés, unsuccessfully restraining their envy. Then I would boisterously ask him about his purple belt in karate in a vain attempt to let everyone know that his excellence exceeds the arena of academia, that this humble prodigy can also break boards. Perhaps I might have found a transition to remind them that he led his basketball squad in scoring and rebounding, making him the most valuable player on his team, and perhaps, the entire league.

My embellished vision of that day was not to be. Taylor received his awards, but there were other children who earned more. I was a little jealous and, perhaps, somewhat angry. I thought, "Why didn't Taylor try out for the media club? If I had known that he could have been recognized for excellence in reading and received a signed certificate from the governor for finishing ten books from a certain collection of classic literature, he would have read those instead of the silly Harry Potter novels he loves so much." I then blamed Taylor's school because they did not give *me* this information at the beginning of the year; they gave it to the students. All the while I had to hear the same name called out repeatedly, "Angelica Whitley," who must have had an awards checklist that she worked on all year, like a boy scout going for his eagle badge. It became so embarrassingly repetitive, the other students would tiredly and simultaneously chant her name before the presenter could, robbing that particular recognition of its climax. "Angelica Whitley," they would painfully moan, aware that her presence eliminated their chances of ever earning the most prestigious acknowledgements, limiting most of them to the yellow "Field Day Participant" ribbons, plastic citizenship pins, attendance bumper stickers or the Styrofoam dish that a self-proclaimed calligraphy artist carefully inscribed with a Sharpie, "Clean Plate Club," which is the cafeteria's highest distinction and by no means a shallow accomplishment.

I became fixed on a child I recognized from our front yard at home, a tall Italian boy who had recently moved into our neighborhood from Pennsylvania. Two families lived together in the house just down the street, three boys about the ages of Garrett and Taylor, (who were 8 and 11 at the time, respectively) and a teenage, delinquent girl who had recently been released from a juvenile correction facility and was showing no signs of finding that new leaf she was supposed to flip. Eventually, we learned that their house was nothing more than a Southern hideout, protecting them all from an abusive existence they thought they could leave 500 miles behind. The adults in the home were cousins, each nobly salvaging her family by ripping them from the clutches of an abusive husband and father, settling into the ranch house at the end of my preferably quiet cul-de-sac. These three boys had issues of various sorts, and I was very cautious about my children spending unsupervised time with them. I would reluctantly allow moderate interaction, simply because there is such a large population of retired people living nearby who, much to Garrett and Taylor's chagrin, have lost their zeal for stick ball and make-believe sword fighting. My wife Cindy and I always had the new boys come to our home to play where they could be monitored; we never allowed our children to go to their house. Some may think that she and I were being snobs, or at the very least overly protective, but I refuse to take unnecessary chances with my children, regardless of public perception. At any rate, as I became more familiar with them, I sensed the disturbance behind their eyes that I knew too well, and I was not going to deliberately put my two boys in harm's way for the sake of neighborhood harmony. They seemed normal to me on most occasions, but there were times when the make-believe sword duels became real, or the stick ball released a fiery fiend, as if the distant enchanter from Pennsylvania had reassumed his mind control. My children were not to become indirect victims of his abuse, so we discouraged future encounters with the Italian boys who romped and played in the paved circle at the end of Ember Lane.

His name was Trey. He was older than the other children in his class by two years, which became obvious when they marched into the media center; he was at least a head taller than everyone else. His class rigidly sat on the blue carpet in their predetermined rows, all rather obviously and recently threatened about showing any sign of non-conformity to the guests from the outside world. His thick, black, tangled hair blocked any attempt to see his eyes because he stared downward, drawing imaginary doodles with his index finger into the fabric of the flooring. A trained educator could tell that Trey's particular seating location was not left to chance as were those of other children, but it had been carefully selected, directly in front of a teacher with a firm hand and a phony smile. It was also obvious that she was pressing the barrel of a metaphoric pistol against his cerebellum, like a kidnapper does a hostage, daring him to try any of his normally disruptive antics during this sacred event. Several times throughout the proceedings she leaned forward and silently reminded him of her ultimatums, hiding her mouth behind his head from the cluster of grinning parents and relatives gathered across the room. I could tell that he was immune to her whispery warnings. She could not see his face, so she did not know that he was no threat to the ceremonial ambiance that the insincere applause and construction-paper decorations inspired. His mood was somber and withdrawn. Perhaps for the first time all year, the teacher's presence was not necessary, but that did not matter to the ever-vigilant staff. They were at their assigned posts, expecting the unexpected, like the secret service before a presidential visit, keeping an eye on the fourteen-year-old sixth grader.

Throughout the ceremony, even when it was obvious that the speakers could not possibly be describing Trey as they monotonously dropped hints about the identity of each praiseworthy recipient, his countenance would sadden and he would slump when a name other than his own was called. One after another, his frustration mounted. He began subtly throwing his arms into the air in silent protest, like a basketball player to a referee for not calling an obvious foul. Finally I heard his name uttered amidst a long list of others, and I found myself praying that whatever the award was for, it would be the elixir he needed to endure the feelings of inadequacy I watched overcome him. However, what appeared to be around 50 children were also called for the same award, such a large population of the students in attendance that it made the gesture inconsequential; I silently cursed the school for frivolously mass-producing so many tokens of mediocrity, vibrant symbols that meant nothing to the child, teachers, or spectators. The kids were lined up and handed the certificates as they marched slowly by, like orphans with empty bowls awaiting their watered-down potato soup in a Dickens novel. I can not remember what the award was for, something like "Outstanding Bus Rider," but there was no justification, individual praise, or amusing tidbit for Trey and his mother to hear, assuming she were actually in attendance. The award-presenting teachers, who were handing out carrot-orange certificates, continued quickly, rapidly working like army reserves tossing government cheese to hungry natural catastrophe victims. I watched his face as he anonymously walked by the throng of parents with his tacky award in hand. He was obviously not expecting a standing ovation for his citizenship during mass transit, and did not get one. He plopped onto the floor at his assigned spot and continued his downward gaze, but at least this time he could study an orange, summative symbol of his positive contributions to the school. I had completely lost all interest in the teachers' tedious babblings, as if every day of the school year had been better than the one before it, so I watched Trey carefully, vicariously experiencing his disappointment. The teacher behind him sensed it as well, which prompted her to lean forward and whisper something into his ear. The untrained eye might think it was a congratulatory offering, but I knew better. She was repositioning herself, reminding my new neighbor that he was still her hostage for the rest of the ceremony.

I heard the students moan, "Angelica Whitley" in unison a few more times, a spontaneous, collective effort to accept inevitable rejection. I considered it rather ironic to watch them unconsciously forge an impromptu cooperative protest beneath an awning of competition; the inherent natures of the children quietly assumed a unified stance against the humiliation that coincides with the repetitious promotion of one child over the rest. There seemed to be consolation in losing in a group because—this should not alarm—relationships and cooperative support revive and nurture. It occurred to me that the children were innately forming an alliance to overcome the unintentional belittlement. The adults in the room thought it was rude when they chanted Angelica's name, and that it was—for Angelica's sake only.

Mercifully, the festivities ended and the parents and students were quickly shown to their respective exits. I heard Trey's teacher scolding him on my way out when she thought it safe to resume her verbosely authoritative dominance. I turned around and saw him standing but hunched over, about 50 feet away, nose-to-nose with the school employee whose only responsibility for the past ninety minutes had been watching him. Students walked by the pair as if the scene were as common as a water fountain or faded bulletin board. Her hand was on his shoulder, angrily and unsuccessfully trying to dip her face into his sagging and defiant gaze. I do not know if she could tell that he was crying because his hair still drooped into a black veil, but his profile again made it unmistakable. At first I did not understand the reason he was confronted and nearly went over to tell the teacher to leave him alone because his behavior had not at all been disruptive. A closer inspection revealed, however, that she was angry with him for his obvious lack of appreciation. There, in his left hand, I observed what seemed to be a piece of carrot-orange paper, wadded into a shredded, mangled mess, dangling from clinched and trembling fingers.

THE COLDEST RAIN

As a sophomore in high school I was in a competition for the reserve first baseman's position on the varsity baseball team with a junior; a stellar senior occupied the spot, but he had the ability to play outfield, so it was possibly a starting position. I was better than Richard Hemmingway, the junior, in every facet of baseball, but I wasn't cocky or brash about it. I lacked confidence but had athletic ability, which kept me from feeling competition's sting earlier in life. I moved to this new community at the conclusion of my ninth grade year and had spent the past seven months being the new kid. We had no junior varsity team, so it was make the varsity squad or sit at home every afternoon drinking generic soda and eating moon pies, the ones that never mold. However, that was not a realistic possibility. I hit the ball better than nearly everyone else on the team in tryouts and many times better than my foe. He made errors at first base and didn't know the proper footwork or how to respond correctly in game situations; these were second nature to me.

Baseball season began at the end of a difficult junior varsity basketball experience where the new coach had followed his players up from the middle school (where he coached them) to the high school. He made them all first string from the first day of practice; at first we sophomores thought it was simply because he knew their names, but it continued. For all we could tell, he enjoyed the novelty of it. We never really felt that we had a chance to start. He once openly bragged that he was winning with ninth graders even though his tenth grade players were good enough to start as well, but he felt more comfortable with the freshmen because he "knew them better" and trusted them. He was building for the future, as if 10th graders are washed up. During tryouts it was rumored that he had the ninth graders over to his house for a small gathering. They came to school the next day telling everyone who had made the team and who had been cut. Unfortunately, I made the team and sat on the bench. So one might understand that I was seeking redemption in baseball season. I had an extra incentive to make the team; if I didn't, I would have to go home every day after school.

It rained that afternoon in late February when the baseball coach announced the cuts following practice in the gym. Richard, my competition, was seemingly dejected and had conceded defeat. I was trying to be humble and supportive to him. He knew that if I beat him out, he would be cut, and I would suffer the same fate if he somehow made the roster. He was not a bad player, but this differed from basketball season because I didn't feel the bias that I had been fighting since moving to the small town over the summer. The coach seemed fair and did not appear to show favoritism to anyone; I swore that he hated us all, but he hated equally and fairly, which was acceptable to me. He had our brand new uniforms draped over the first row of the wooden bleachers, both the home reds and the away grays, separated by number. There were sixteen uniforms on display and thirty-eight pounding hearts sitting impatiently on the hard gym floor, gazing at them as if they were the only parachutes on a crashing plane.

He called the names of the returning seniors up one at a time, beginning with the all-conference players and working downward. After that, there were nine uniforms left. Number 31 was still there; it was the number I wore the previous summer in Babe Ruth when I led the city in hitting with an even .500 batting average. He called the returning juniors from the previous year's team; all four of them selected a uniform and returned to the crowd, holding their numbers up for admirers to see. Five uniforms left, and my number was still available. I calmed myself by remembering that I had also earned a gold glove in the city league seven months earlier for going twenty-two games at first base without an error. However, even those numbers weren't enough to make the all-star team; I fell back into panic mode. The summer league all-star coach selected the first baseman off the team he managed during the regular season, his son's best friend, who had seven errors and hit below .300. I was new to the city then and I supposed being a native counted for something, so I pouted for a few days until I became comfortable with this newest frustration. Two more juniors' names were called, which left only three uniforms. I was getting nervous, but I figured he would give the remaining three to sophomores like me.

"Richard Hemmingway!" He angrily bellowed in the same frequency he used to summon the rest of his team. Richard screamed like a Confederate soldier and pumped his fist into the air. I frantically tried to interpret the meaning of this unexpected and shocking turn. Rejection burned my face, but there were two more numbers left; 31, however, was not available. Richard had it hanging from his extended arms above his face as if he was sending a distress signal with it. He was a matador and I the lowly bull, swinging the home red jersey before me and snatching it away while stabbing me in the back. By the time I regained my composure, the remaining two jerseys were gone and the coach was into his "thanks for coming out" speech. I hated this town that had hated me since my arrival.

I had no way of knowing that later in the spring the varsity baseball coach would be accused of accepting bribes, like the alleged set of radial tires given to him by businessman Alan Hemmingway, the local Firestone dealer, reportedly put on the coach's truck a few days after his son made the team. These events were in the future and were of no comfort to the fifteen-year-old boy who walked home in the rain, with his first baseman's mitt tucked under his arm, looking upward into a pelting shower and crying steaming tears from an oft-beaten heart, as the indifferent, rush-hour traffic whisked by.

I wish that I had known at that particular time that I would be the starting first baseman for the next two years, my junior and senior seasons and that we would lose only two regular-season games during the time I played. I would go on to win meaningless awards and honors both as a student and an athlete, culminating in a college scholarship in football. I advanced to the next level, motivated by accolades and glory, until I met the inevitable humiliation of falling victim to the competitive hierarchy. It was nothing personal; it happens to every athlete eventually. Most would tell you that it was worth it, something that might be superciliously true for those who experienced some degree of success (at the expense of others) during the process. But if you ask me which had the biggest impact on my life, I will tell you that getting cut from my high school baseball team when I was a sophomore affected me more than any recognition or trophy. As I matured, I learned to find little celebrity or prestige at the cost of another's dignity, even if I won plaques or golden statues to signify these accomplishments. Perhaps these became meaningless to me because rewards require a pondering of the past and I try not to visit that place too often. I quickly packaged my plaques and trophies in a cardboard vault and eventually lost them all to the attic. The sting of defeat, the indignation of being labeled inferior or simply not good enough, never fit into that box. It remains engrained into my self-image and I have learned to accept it. Perhaps its impact is nothing more than a byproduct of my tainted childhood, but I have seen its effect on others. It is strange that the bitterness of rejection never leaves your mouth, while glory's sweetness fades like flavor in cheap bubble gum.

TAXED ELITISM

If one ever doubts the hold competition has on our schools, try suggesting that all elitist programs (those that are selective and deny participation through a screening process) are removed. Immediately advocates of school-sponsored athletics and exclusive clubs will argue that all students have the opportunity to join if they are willing to work hard enough. However, if seventeen athletes worked equally hard for sixteen jerseys, how would the coach determine who does not get one? The sixteen players who give him the best chance of winning would don jerseys, and the lone child who was deemed less equipped to help accomplish this goal would be cut. If an educator suggests that honor societies are selected objectively, he or she is delusional. Grades are at best subjective interpretations, where teachers are influenced by a variety of factors not affiliated with pure academic measurement, probably because there is no such thing. Then there are character statements and interviews that are more about hype than substance. Local politics and personal biases are impossible to screen fairly. I have observed a committee discussing unsubstantiated rumors about a child's morality. I have also witnessed parents strong-arm principals into adding a name to the roster moments before the induction ceremony. I remember the principal saying, "I am not losing my job over this." Then there is the child who missed the cut by a tenth of a percentage point on the rubric, based on the formula the committee concocted to divert responsibility from themselves.

Athletics have many positive qualities, but to experience them, one must examine the effect they have on successful participants, not those who were cut or pushed to the end of the bench. Because coaches rarely see their success as anything other than winning, the school or its employee have little to do with the positive side effects that accidentally occur during the course of the season. Coaches are not to blame, however, because losing is a primary reason many are fired. The National Federation of State High School Associations (NFHS) suggests that these elitist activities are beneficial for the following reasons: (1) activities support the academic mission of the school, (2) activities are inherently educational, and (3) activities foster success later in life.[1] It seems rather evident that NFSH is not referring to the benefits for the athletes who were cut or those who made the team but discovered that winning was more important than their opportunity to play. The focus here is on the successful, not those who are publicly told to leave the practice facility, that they were not good enough. Notice that the three statements are theoretical, widely-accepted assumptions that cannot be measured or objectively evaluated. They use words like "success" that are without concrete definition and based on one's perspective. Strangely enough, it seems that the benefits of athletics as stated by NFSH are more applicable to curricular activities where winning is not a priority.

How important, then, is winning to the children who make the team? According to a survey conducted by the Sporting Goods Manufacturers Association, "having fun" was the number one reason that girls and boys participate in high school sports. Conversely, a lack of fun was the number one reason they dropped out or quit. "Unfortunately, compelling evidence suggests that, for many children, the pressures associated with sports produce low self-esteem, excessive anxiety, and aggressive behavior. Children may eventually experience 'sports burnout' and develop a lifelong avoidance of physical activity."[2] Is it a coincidence that, as previously stated by Orlick, that 80 to 90 percent of sports participants drop out by the age of fifteen, when competition and winning are intensified on the high school level? Could competition and the lust for winning take the fun out of sports, thus depriving a vast majority of the aesthetic academic development that the NFSH holds so sacred? Remarkably,

"Winning was not seen as a major benefit of sports by young people who participate—it was ranked No. 8 by the boys and No. 12 by the girls."[3] The report added that intrinsic rewards outweighed the extrinsic ones, the most significant reward being "self knowledge."

If it is not a primary factor for the students, it must be important to the grown ups. Adults are primarily responsible for the negative impact of competition on children, "particularly parents and coaches. Lip-service is paid to sportsmanship and having fun, but rewards are reserved for winning."[4] Schools should not be platforms for adults to quench their lust for winning by corrupting the purity of athletics by putting winning above the other positive qualities schools promote as the benefits of athletics. As long as cutting is practiced, winning is the lone objective, and interest and participation dramatically decreases as students progress through schools, schools are not fostering their missions or building future success as the NFSH proclaims. They are doing just the opposite.

The laws that protect children from discrimination of this nature reveal two things about our culture: first, competition is also ingrained into our laws; second, our laws are contradictory. Every state in the nation prohibits discrimination based on race, creed, religion, gender, and disability. Assuming that child abuse is not a disability because the schools seem to shun its existence or consider it someone else's problem, then the adherence to a competitive selection process is fundamentally based on a system of fairness and accountability. Courts have allowed schools flexibility in formulating eligibility requirements for extra-curricular activities. In *Public School Law,* it explains that "selection can be based on selective judgments, and as long as fair procedures are uniformly applied, courts will not disturb such decisions."[5] The Wisconsin Department of Public Instruction (Wisconsin DPI) explains this practice a little more concretely:

> Students may not be denied the opportunity to try out for a team or be excluded from a team based on a disability. However, decisions regarding the selection of team members . . . involve the exercise of judgment and a great degree of discretion by the coach.[6]

The coach cannot deny students from trying out, but his or her selection is dependent upon a "great degree of discretion." The fallacy here that shows how we are so mired in competition our laws and standards pertaining to child development are paradoxical. First, the assumption that all children are equal is at the heart of competition, probably because the American society is also steeped in the concept of fairness as a premise. Secondly, there is no way to assure that the coach's "discretion" is consistent with the spirit of discrimination laws. The wording of that phrase in the Wisconsin DPI's bylaws legally erases the overarching statement that protects children from discrimination if the desired involvement is an elitist, extra-curricular activity. Coaches want to win, not lead sweaty campaigns of self-discovery.

THE SEEDLING

Wade, eight years old, was a bit shy but eager to try basketball in his community recreational league. It was the first practice since the children were divided into teams; they were warming up when the coach called them all together. Little Wade hustled over while some remained behind, ignoring his whistle and continuing to shoot. Not Wade however, who sat right in front of the coach, who stood gazing over him at the boys still on the court. He called the stragglers by name until the last child eventually settled on the hardwood floor at his feet. After a brief welcome and introduction, the seven boys were sent out onto the court with a gallery of wide-eyed parents watching closely. Coach Jones was a police officer whose son was predetermined to be the star of the team, which is probably why he coached. He called the names of five boys and had them stand. Wade and the other boy, whose names the coach didn't know, were told to sit on the bench and listen. He turned to address his son and the four teammates standing at mid court, awaiting the opportunity to display their basketball talents. "You guys are my starting five," he shouted with absolute certainty, even though he had not seen as much as a lay-up from the other two. He then turned to Wade and the other boy and said confidently, "You are my bench. Your job is to give these players (pointing to the starting five) some rest." Five of the parents present continued watching with smug smiles, while two dads became very uneasy.

After about twenty minutes of drills, he decided to scrimmage. Again he called out his starting five, and again, he placed Wade on the bench with the other nameless boy. He discussed the offense and the defense in a voice so low that parents nor the two players on the bench could hear. When ready to scrimmage, he called his daughter and another son onto the court, both a few years older than the team members. Two other fathers joined the coach and his offspring, who would scrimmage the starting five for the next twenty minutes until the practice time expired. Wade sat on the sideline with his new buddy, picking at his Nikes, already accepting his role as a second-tier player. His father restrained himself until the coach concluded his post-practice speech, when he talked about playing as a team and "winning a bunch of games this year." The five sweaty kids, and the two who were dry, sprinted to their awaiting parents. Wade didn't have to run far, because I, his father, was half way to center court to talk to the coach of the third and fourth grade team.

Although I never call my son "Wade" unless to conceal his identity for dramatic effect as is this case, Taylor and I have the same middle name. I understood that any public rant would only embarrass him further, but a father can only watch so much when his child is being openly sacrificed to build others, especially when that father knows firsthand how devastating rejection can be. I was furious as I advocated for Taylor and the nameless child, whose father had stormed out of the gym with the intention of removing him from the team. I suppose I was a bit animated; it was during my somewhat controlled, low-volumed tirade that he felt it necessary to inform me of his position as a public servant in law enforcement. I explained how he ridiculed the two kids and accused him of being the president of the "daddy-ball" league.

In retrospect, the coach took the criticism well and I narrowly avoided arrest; he developed the two benchwarmers by giving them a generous amount of playing time throughout the year. In fact, Taylor played as much as anyone else. They lost every game, and Taylor was not very good, but the others weren't either. Three years later, Coach Jones selected Taylor in the draft (another ploy established for the adults' amusement more than the children's) as a sixth grader, and finally found those wins he was seeking. Taylor Wade had become one of the tallest children in his grade. I have already mentioned Taylor's accomplishments, leader of the entire league in scoring and rebounding. Taylor did not care about that, he just loved to play basketball with his friends.

Perhaps this is the story I would not have been able to tell if Coach Jones's blinding ambition to win had not been addressed three years earlier. When we allow winning to drive us, we ignore potential in lieu of instant gratification. The buds are not fed and the flowers never blossom, simply because the coach will not get glory and credit when and if they do. I suppose I do not blame the coach because he too is a product of a competitive society. Many coaches are grown men using grade schoolers to feed egos made hungry by their own failures because feelings of athletic inadequacy still haunt them. Middle-aged adults, yelling at referees, scouting and drafting players at "skills day," and pumping fists into the air as their teams run up the score on other children, are competition's fools. They rejoice, regain composure to humbly congratulate the other coach, the loser who finds consolation in the bitter yet insincere reminder that it isn't important who wins but how the game is played. While children from both teams, unaffected by the scoreboard, run for the canned drinks and oatmeal cakes that the smiling team moms pull from coolers.

Coach Jones revealed true character for seeing how winning is not the primary goal and by putting things back into perspective, learning that children are not pawns as much as they are seedlings. Treat them as game pieces and they are gradually removed from the board unnoticeably while the more "important" pieces remain until they too are gone. Nurture them when they are young and they might develop into trees that stands strong and proud, whose presence increases each year, and whose branches shade fathers and coaches, who in their old age, are too weak and tired to handle the heat of the competitive sun.

CANDLES AND CAMERAS

Athletics in high school is where elitism is most visibly manifested, but it occurs on all levels. I witnessed high school baseball players preparing for a game from my classroom window; students who were supposed to be in my English class taking a test, were taking batting practice instead. I saw a 2–9 football team leave campus on a Friday morning to travel five hours each way in a chartered bus to play a football game. The bus alone cost the team over $600. More teams were added to the playoff brackets because the state's athletic association gets twenty percent of the revenues from every playoff game. That particular game cost the school about $1100 to lose 42–6, but they were compensated with 40 percent of the gate, which totaled about $440. The difference came out of the school's budget. But when administrators speak to faculties, they bellow, "academics come first," and I sincerely believe they think it is so because they decree it. Advocates for school-sponsored athletic competition rightly say that kids learn teamwork, camaraderie, and see the relationship between success and hard work. So do children in classrooms if managed properly.

Resilient environments do not endorse Darwinistic cutting, battles for playing time, or the hostile desire to humiliate rival children. But until classrooms are operating properly, perhaps the advocates are right. Maybe basketball is the only reason Billy-Bob goes to school, but it does not have to be. He needs the sport to give him self-worth and identity, things a cooperative classroom is more than equipped to handle. In fact, it is rather sad when we allow a sport to define Billy Bob, when his participation in that sport is likely to end in high school. What does he have then? Has his school served him or lulled him into the trance of a temporary oasis? In the spirit of the new order others before me propose, it is only assumable that elitist programs hinder overall progress and give access to a few at the expense of denying access to others. This is not in the spirit of public education. Therefore, the first step in creating pure schools that foster resiliency is to take a look at the elitist clubs and teams and either find a way to open them to all who are interested when they are age appropriate, or do away with them altogether. There is no way to select children for a club or team without subjectivity and bias. Processes that reveal corruption and bias have already been illustrated that show how this adversely affects the child by attacking his or her self worth. No child should feel the sting of getting cut at school by being told that he or she is not good enough, regardless of the coach's record or the group's reputation.

Consider the abused and neglected child who reaches out beyond his cocoon and courageously seeks the self-redemption that participation on a team would instill. He sheepishly goes through the routines that the others know well. He integrates with peers and, perhaps, begins a new friendship or two. He was not encouraged to go out by anyone, but he does, fearing ridicule and dreaming of the prestige that coincides with wearing the uniform. He is cut. There is no support system to catch him when he falls back into his lair, where he and others think he belongs, and from which he should never have ventured. Elitist competition threatens resiliency and nearly destroys the children who bear the weight of abuse and neglect. Anti-discrimination laws that save others from biases do not protect abused children, so they travel this road alone.

It is always good when you can discriminate against children and stand behind an official, un-reproachable name with the words like "National," and "Honor," in the title, so established that it can even be phrased as an acronym to be even more intimidating. In this example, I am referring to the National Junior Honor Society, (NJHS), probably formed because the National Honor Society did not identify the elite soon enough. Although their requirements seem as concrete as possible, usually a 3.5 grade point average and teacher-supervised rankings in several other areas that are compiled and calculated on a rubric. Then the sum of the parts is divided by the number of areas observed, providing the evaluators with a concrete, measurable scale score that is seemingly indisputable. In some cases, it is a fraction of a percentage point that disqualifies an applicant. If the school chooses not to use a point system, the student is subject to NJHS committee voting. It is my observation in education that the more documentation you need to qualify a decision, the more subjective it probably is. However, before this prestigious seventh grade academic judgment day, all students in the school who maintain that pre-established grade point average are notified. The child then goes on a self-promoting scavenger hunt, compiling a resume or portfolio that covers mastery of the other four areas: service, leadership, character, and citizenship. The entire process is extremely flawed for a variety of reasons.

First, some students are sought out and encouraged to apply for admission, only to be rejected by the club or organization a few weeks later. Secondly, the grade point averages students post are tainted because teacher grades are subjective. There are huge inconsistencies from one teacher to another in grading, teaching style, fairness, and ability to develop resilient classroom climates. Third, homework grades are not fair due to variations in parental assistance, the presence of a home computer and other resources, and the existence of an environment conducive to learning. Fourth, service is described by most middle school websites as involvement with an organization like scouting or a church youth group. Abused and neglected children would love to participate in these activities. However, the issue becomes a fear of asking mom for a ride to a church they don't attend or getting $25 from Dad for scout dues. Leadership is very difficult when a child is not supported at home.

Abused kids are in survival mode, not parade mode. Character and citizenship may be questioned because teachers may observe awkward social skills, emotional reactions, or disciplinary issues. They are recruited because, miraculously, they hold a 3.5 grade point average or better and must be asked because that is the initial criteria of the organization, even though members and advisors may find the candidate's possibilities of actually being inducted rather remote. So the child is recruited and given the opportunity to sniff acceptance and belonging momentarily, until the inviting host slams the familiar door of rejection into their hopeful eyes. In some cases the denied student is later required to sit in an assembly and watch the fortunate few light candles to the flashes of their parents' cameras and hear the applause that characterizes glory and acceptance, while the abused and neglected student—who achieved something more miraculous than anyone on the stage—enviously watches from the audience.

As seemingly obvious the reasons for having selective activities in public schools, there are undoubtedly stronger reasons for changing or eliminating them. If "No Child Left Behind" is nothing but a cliché, or is applicable only to test scores, then it reflects the shallow approaches of educational leadership on the highest level. If we are to take its meaning literally, then leaders should apply it to all facets of education. If participation in athletic events is so rich in educational value, then it should be rationalized why so many students are denied the opportunity to participate. There must be no gaps or holes in the nets we hang to protect our children who take the chance on the high wire. We must consider the tragic cruelty of the screening processes and what rejection does to the development of self-esteem. Even if all children had similar backgrounds and systems of support, there is something inherently wrong with the approach to athletics in schools, once adults mix the need for competition and lust for winning into the equation. All one needs to do is focus on the losers and not the winners, the rejected in lieu of the honored, and it becomes obvious. Follow a child home in the rain after getting cut from his baseball team and enter the doors of an abusive home. Share his pain for a moment, then apply it to the whole. Winning is expensive.

From this perspective, where we promote the strong at the expense of the weak, our leaders have chosen a philosophy much closer to the aforementioned Hitler and Darwin than those of Martin Luther King Jr. or Gandhi. A purist might say that education reform involving selective organizations calls for nothing short of disbanding these programs. However, there are reasonable solutions. Our schools are not going to abandon competitive athletics because the school is a product of the society that supports it. Parents and adults will continue to contaminate athletics by injecting without question an animalistic lust for winning. But it does not have to be a product of the school curriculum, sapping funds and distorting priorities. With younger children, the community forms youth leagues because there are no competitive school athletics at that time; athletic teams are not needed to promote, enhance, or supplement elementary schools. Yet most civic organizations create several teams to facilitate all children who are interested at each age level. If this method was as prevalent on the middle school and, yes, high school levels, then might we have more children participating at the high school level? This would be an excellent tool to link the school with the community Lion's Club or YMCA. The school could offer its resources, gym and fields, and even transportation in some cases. The civic groups could get academic vouchers from the schools that qualify the student/athlete and offer its resources to the school. Local businesses or individuals could sponsor teams. The school and the civic organization could easily raise the money spent on athletics. Admission to events from a larger population of interested parties, donations, and fund-raisers could easily cover the expenses. More importantly, monies normally designated for athletics could be used to provide programs for *all* students while offering *all* students the opportunity to participate in athletics.

Parents can have their honor societies and other clubs of distinction, but if they want the club to motivate and inspire, then leave its doors open. Individualize the requirements for admission so a child can showcase strengths, not deficiencies that may be beyond his or her control. If honor society members are to be real leaders, then instead of rejecting fellow students, cooperatively identify areas in which improvement is necessary, and then, collectively, make it their missions to get them into the organization by assisting them. No rejections, just a "Not yet, but we will help you get there." Burn candles for others, not ourselves. Make the goal of the honor society not the acceptance, but the network of people helping others to achieve honor status by establishing criteria that give every student who is interested a fair opportunity to become a member. This is how competition becomes cooperation. This is how we facilitate children who have little support or confidence.

I am not delusional. I realize that our system is too mesmerized by blind tradition to change now. This is our reality. It would be disobedient and blasphemous to promote another way. It would be considered a threat to something people hold sacred, even if they do not know why. A leader who suggests any modification to these elitist activities would be figuratively crucified like the one who was literally, like the other great leaders who were similarly martyred by those who lit candles for themselves in an ignorant world.

NOTES

1. "The Case for High School Activities," *National Federation of State High School Associates* 2003 <http://www.nfhs.org/web/2004/01/the_case_for_high_school_activities.aspx> (28 March 2006).
2. Jon Hellstedt, "Kids, Parents and Sport: Some Questions and Answers. *The Physician and Sportsmedicine* 16, no. 4, (April, 1988): 59–71.
3. *Public School Laws of North Carolina* (Charlottesville, VA: LexisNexis, 2001): 25.
4. Hellstedt, "Kids, Parents and Sport."
5. Nelda H. Cameron-McCabe, Martha M. McCarthy and Stephen B.Thomas, *Public School Law.* (Boston: Pearson, 2004): 136.
6. Wisconsin Department of Public Instruction, 1997, <http://www.dpi.wi. giov./sped/pdf/athletics.pdf> (26 March 2006): 18.

Chapter Five

The Ugly Underbelly of Competition

"In academe, I see competition and, still, white man elitism."

—Maxine Greene, *A Light in Dark Times*

WITHOUT NETS

Educational activist Alfie Kohn openly criticizes the widely practiced quick fix of dangling carrots to motivate students. He challenges the apple pie cornerstones of the American fabric and in doing so, reveals the virus that stigmatizes many educational reform movements. His teachings do not directly address the issues surrounding child abuse so the significance of its parallel with the subject will not be made immediately, but his points are paramount in exposing a cultural obsession that must be examined and corrected before we even attempt to reach all students as magically mandated by federal legislation. He states:

> There is a time to admire the grace and persuasive power of an influential idea, and there is a time to fear its hold over us. The time to worry is when the idea is so widely shared that we no longer even question it, when it is so deeply rooted that it feels to us like plain common sense. At the point when objections are not answered anymore because they are no longer even raised, we are not in control: we do not have the idea; it has us.[1]

To assume that politicians, so steeped in the rhetoric of their trade and the fallacious concepts they associate with progress, could have anything to do with a successful educational reform movement is ludicrous. Presidents and governors are perhaps the last people in the nation who would be qualified to question competition's impact on the common man, more specifically, the abused child. They are survivors of a competitive environment who must endorse this accepted American process because it gives them credibility and public authority; in fact, it made them who and what they are. The politics of their party affiliation and budgetary concerns define what is needed and acceptable. They feed on statistical manipulation and four-year, cyclical posturing instead of true, bottom-up reform, which is the only way schools will collectively improve and why few, if any, reform movements over the past several decades have succeeded (unless you believe the governmental education advisors' manipulated statistics). Reform will be difficult to accomplish until our politicians and local school boards become willing to part with power and admit that their expertise is limited. They need to let the professionals who have experience and educational backgrounds push the movement and they need to fund it properly, but politicians did not rise to their lofty perches by relinquishing power. Education in our country is retarded by all who profess to know better than the professionals within the walls of the schools. Their lack of understanding is why they need statistical data (as provided by high-stakes testing) to justify their conjectures and issue self-credit for the actions of those performing well on tests, despite bureaucratic distractions.

If the national and state politicians were not enough to thwart educational reform, we give a tremendous amount of authority to local school boards. The only real policing of ethical practices and sound decision-making comes from the voters and the local media. However, in rural counties there is no media, or the newspaper is not much more than a glorified bulletin board, so the public is not informed about school board activities or able to monitor ethics carefully. In essence, there is a weak system of accountability. Board meetings can become a charade of rhetoric while the decisions that reveal their incapacity for the job, or their lack of knowledge about its responsibilities, are hidden in "closed session" meetings or pinned behind the curtain of "personnel matters." Factions form within the board and values are compromised for supporting votes on unrelated issues. In essence, the board is formed by many who ran unopposed or campaign success that fell to the candidate who cluttered the county with the loudest signs. According to William T. Harris, the U.S. Commissioner of Education in 1892, there are three common types of school board members:

> First, the businessmen chosen from the class of merchants, bankers, and manufacturers, or professional men who have no personal ends to serve and no special cause to plead. Second, there are the men representing the element of reform or change, honest and well-meaning but prone to an unbalanced judgment. A third class of men . . . is the self-seeking or selfish man.[2]

It has been my experience that this hundred-year-old description has adequate relevance in the twenty-first century. Is this a governing body that might inadvertently bring elements of adult society and the business models into its educational decision-making? To suggest that there are many "cooks stirring the broth" is an understatement; each one seasoning the soup to his liking without purposefully considering the fact that the meal being prepared is for children.

The fact that competition has been instrumental in the United States' rise to global respectability is attributed to the need to implement it as a key component in most hidden curricula. One must also acknowledge that it has pulsed through the veins of our capitalistic society since the industrial revolution over 100 years ago. We evaluate one another by our occupations and, ultimately, the assumed salary that such a position commands. The dollar has become the measuring stick of success and failure in most circles. The awards I envisioned my son carrying home were significant to me because the underlying assumption is that they would one day translate into prosperity. Since I too am the product of a system so steeped in competition that its political leaders think it is a basis for motivation and reform, I enjoyed the vicarious and fleeting moment of victory at the awards ceremony. I did not notice or care how the my sons rise from mediocrity to elitism at the expense of the 11-year-old classmates (and one older child) would affect them, those clutching their meaningless carrots with one hand and embracing their humiliation with the other. Competition is a blindness that has distorted priorities because it feeds egos in the same manner greed does corruption. It is a pernicious habit that feasts beneath the guise of wholesomeness and character development.

I take comfort in the fact that striving for material wealth and fame at the expense of others has been a trap into which men have fallen for thousands of years. In Plato's *Republic*, during a conversation with Adeimantus around 400 B.C., Socrates discusses the value of having businessmen and politically-ambitious individuals involved in the education of children:

> Adeimantus: A somewhat squalid fellow, who makes a profit from everything and hoards it—the sort the majority admires. Is not this the man who resembles such a constitution?
>
> Socrates: That's my opinion, anyway. At any rate, money is valued above everything by both the city and the man.
>
> Adeimantus: I don't suppose that such a man pays any attention to education.
>
> Socrates: Not in my view, for, if he did, he wouldn't have chosen a blind leader (reference to Plutus, the god of wealth, who is blind) for his chorus and honored him most.

It was my son's awards ceremony that brought prophetic truths about competition into focus for me. How readily I, an educator, accepted the dismantling of these other children as a necessary ingredient in Taylor's educational development proved that the standards by which we measure and weigh adults had seeped into the developmental years of children. Not only does this happen, but we accept and embrace it. We celebrate it.

In relation to the abused child, what exactly is endorsed when people support the competitive curriculum in schools? Linking school competition and child abuse, considering the issuance of grades is a form of competitive measurement, studies have determined that reports of child abuse double after report cards are sent home.[3] Abused children's grades often hold intensified significance to the parents because they have low self-esteem, which causes them to view the child's actions as psychological extensions of themselves. They interpret the child's poor performance with their own inadequacies and failures. "Thus, the poor report card grades serve as a 'trigger' for the abusive parent's violence toward the child."[4] In Florida, a father was sentenced to twenty-five years in prison for raping his eight-year-old daughter for bringing home a bad report card. According to the *Sun Sentinel*, he threatened to rape her 400 times if she came home with a single bad report card.[5]

The most devastation, as previously stated, occurs when there is not support. When I watched an educator chastise an abused child because he was not appreciative of an insulting recognition, I realized that few beyond the children of abuse have the power to see through or dismantle their veils. They have not the footing to compete with my son or others whose parents support them, empowering them to take chances without fear of failure. As previously documented, their brains are operating in an entirely different mode than those of other children. I considered the other papers Trey must get throughout the year from teachers, such as poor report cards, discipline referrals, notes to his mother, and failing graded assignments. He has little positive support at home because the entire family is stuck in survival mode, and the communication and feedback he gets from school slams his self-esteem again and again. Without consistent, positive parental guidance, the child stays in his comfort zone and does not take the structured risks others take. He does not have the support to rebound from shock. But we measure them as if all our children develop on an equal plane. Is Trey going to take the chances that lead to learning and success that my son Taylor takes? Does anyone really believe that teachers have the same expectations and strive to offer Trey the same opportunities as the others? Are teachers able to recognize the source of Trey's burdens? Do they know how to help overcome them?

A few years after their infancy, children are unwillingly placed upon the competitive high wire and forced to conform to this adult idealism; some children waltz out onto the wire with nets below and others drearily and shakily tread forth knowing the only thing beneath them is the sting of the pavement. In some ways they are aware that the parents (of the children with nets) want them to fall in order to glorify their own. The stands below are full of these blindly-accepting adults, who are in attendance solely to reap the fruits of victory. These intelligent, well-intending grown ups have been conditioned by surviving the same competitive screening and do not feel guilt, shame, or even sincere compassion for the losers. We do not question this circus because it has a hundred-year history; we simply applaud the triumphs and temporarily pity the failures with insincere pats on the back as we guide them away. But everybody loves the winners, who are shouldered out of the arena while the losers tend to their bruises alone, fading into a world of darkness, pain, and anonymity until they are heard from no more.

This is not to suggest that *winning* is without consequence. In fact, it simply increases expectations and places the child in more competitive arenas. The issue of motivation is one that will be explored in more detail; however, it is significant to note that parental pressures can be much more severe regarding children whom others may envy. Pressure to maintain lofty standards can also be concentrated. Illinois' New Trier High School, one of the nations top performing schools, the competitive atmosphere is so intense that "hyperambitious students carry calculators to compute their up-to-the-minute GPAs."[6] Social scientist Chris Argyris has studied why smart people have difficulty learning in the work settings. He concludes they have so much invested in their cognitive development in proving what they know and hiding weaknesses, that learning becomes secondary to appearance and image.[7] He quotes Deming who began a meeting with state school department heads by saying, "We've been sold down the river by competition."[8] Victories, or the unquenchable thirst for them, guide the student, who is nothing more than a participant in a pyramiding eternity of competitive levels, with no genuine satisfaction until there are none left to beat. In essence, they rise until they are ultimately defeated themselves, like the fever that consumes the gambler who outplays his win streak. So there are a myriad of losers and only a few winners, and the losses hurt more than the triumphs help.

THE SACRED COW

America is a society so deeply rooted in competition that people rarely ever question its effects on child development. Competition is anything that separates the successful from the unsuccessful, a situation in which some are celebrated by the failure of others. Athletic teams on television dominate the airwaves every weekend. In our communities, parents of eight-year-old children scream bitter insults to umpires and coaches from weather-stained bleachers. Parents paint the faces of their four-year-old daughters and parade them down runways, teaching them to seductively stare at the judges like Bourbon Street hookers. Adults pressure children from the time they are able to bounce a ball and read their names. Children in schools across the nation are eliminated from spelling and geography bees, showing them that competition has no boundaries. We build 100,000 seat football stadiums so athletes, who would not ordinarily qualify for admission, can help the alma maters of fattened alumni humiliate rival universities. Children who have correct answers stretch their arms into the air, hoping that the teacher will call on them and ignore the others.

In *The Moral and Spiritual Crisis in Education*, David Purpel demeans the economic view of public education by attacking the reform movements that have misguided vision at their cores. He shows how hierarchy, order, and competition are antithetical to "educational values of free inquiry, the development of a critical and creative consciousness, and the struggle for meaning."[9] It is rather alarming that many of the federal interventions into American education were spawned by a desire to compete on a global scale. Education has become a governmental tool, in principle, used to preserve national and economic security. The pressure that politicians place on educators creates a tense environment that does not just trickle down into the classrooms—it is magnified there. Many think competition is needed to bring out the best in an individual or team. It is what makes life interesting or meaningful.

Alfie Kohn has emerged as a top educational theorist and reformist who attacks accepted notions about competition by breaking the topic into four widely accepted myths, something he calls the four legs of the sacred cow of competition. All are influenced by a misinterpretation of Darwin's theory of natural selection, in which only the strongest (most competitive) emerge victorious.

The first myth, "Competition is inevitable," suggests that the spirit of competition is a part of human nature. It is, as mentioned, so ingrained into our society that its citizens assume it is natural because Americans are reacting to the competitive nature of their culture as early as they can remember. "Life is viewed as an arena where competition is both inevitable and desirable."[10] In the United States, we often assume that the desperate quest to triumph over others is a universal human condition. But in 1937, Margaret Mead and her colleagues found that competition was virtually unknown to the Zuni and Iroquois in North America and to the Bathonga of South America. Since then, cross-cultural observers have confirmed that our society is the exception rather than the rule.[11]

Two American primatologists recently challenged the current, accepted theory that competition is the driving force of social behavior in primates, both human and non-human. Paul Garber and Robert Sussman made the following conclusion after extensive research on primates: "In place of the 'aggression-competition-reconciliation model' of primate sociality, the researchers offer a new theory that recognizes cooperation and affiliation as the species' primary social behaviors."[12]

The second myth is "Competition keeps productivity high and is necessary for excellence." Many assume that success is the product of competition. Success does not need competition, but competition is dependent upon success and failure. A group of children accomplishing a task together, utilizing teamwork and effort, is an example of success without competition. For example, honor societies that help those who seek admittance accomplish its requirements without measurement, only acceptance. What is more honorable than that?

Kohn cites several studies that confirm his condemnation of the assumption that there is a positive correlation between competition and achievement. He references Robert Helmreich of the University of Texas and his colleagues who conducted studies in various occupational models to determine if competition has a positive effect on achievement. Each study produced a negative correlation between the two factors."[13] Kohn analyzed 122 studies on this topic and found that 101 failed to reflect a positive relationship between achievement and competitiveness. It was also determined that cooperation led to higher levels of achievement in sixty-five of the studies.[14]

"Recreation requires competition" is the third myth. Children are often pitted against one another in gyms and on fields where the objective is to have one group defeat the other. Sports psychologist Terry Orlick observes:

> For many children competitive sports operate as a failure factory that not only eliminates the 'bad ones' but also turns off many of the 'good ones'. . . . In North America it is not uncommon for us to lose from 80 to 90 percent of our registered organized-sports participants by fifteen years of age.[15]

The solution requires a look into the component parts of play, and then filtering out the competitive elements. All games simply require achieving a goal by overcoming some obstacle. Nowhere is it written that the obstacle must be other people. Referring to Orlick's suggested example, imagine musical chairs if all participants remained in the game and each time a chair was removed until everyone was trying to find a way to sit on one chair. There are no losers, no sidelines for those who failed to watch the fun, only a cooperative attempt to overcome an obstacle of increasing difficulty.

The fourth and final myth is "Competition builds character." If competition indeed builds character, then one should examine why humans feel the need to compete. Douglas Kellner suggests that this need is nothing more than a modernistic search for identity, which happens to be at the expense of others. "Identity today becomes a freely-chosen game, a theatrical presentation of the self."[16] In other words, winning is actually not intending to demean the opponent(s), but it most certainly is a side effect that has not been carefully considered. Trying to outperform others is harmful because most lose most of the time. In the business world, eleven applicants may vie for one job. In the sports world, thirty-two National Football League teams claw it out each year for one Lombardi trophy. In the classroom, 15 children raise hands to give the teacher one answer. On the playgrounds, several children eerily prophesize their fates as they compete for one position in a game of "King of the Hill."

Basically, competition and rewards thwart cooperative learning because it transforms others from a supportive resource to a rival. Renowned statistical consultant Dr. W. Edward Deming discusses the impact of weaving the prevailing system of business management into our schools. He describes it the following way:

> The machine world of teachers in control, students dependent on teachers' approval, and learning defined as getting an A on the test. Most of us developed our survival skills for industrial-age institutions in first and second grade. We learned how to please the teacher, as we would later learn how to please our boss. We learned how to avoid wrong answers and raise our hands when we knew the right answer, habits that would later shape the ongoing organizational dance of avoiding blame and seeking credit for successes. We learned how to be quiet when we felt lost, which is why no one questions the boss in the official meeting, even when he or she makes no sense.[17]

James Austin explains the discrepancy at the core of what we know and what we feel in an article called "Alternatives to Competition in Music Education" which appeared in *Education Digest.* He says:

> The large gap between research findings and our intuitive beliefs on this matter might be explained as a different perspective. Competition connoisseurs are naturally drawn to the excitement and thrill of victory that surround extraordinary performances and winning performers. Researchers, on the other hand, generally concern themselves with larger populations that include not only elite performers but also average and struggling performers who often flounder under competitive conditions and bring the average performance score back down to earth in achievement studies.[18]

The threat of competition affects one's closeness to colleagues at work, our recreation and leisure activities, our familial affections, and our fellow students at school. In every human arena there is documentation to suggest that the ill effects of competition, many times preventing the group from achieving the objective that brought them together, have tainted relationships. Ridding ourselves of the handicapping cancer that has embedded itself into the American culture, and is guarded by Darwinian fallacies held sacred by so many, is not going to easily happen. Leaders must begin by re-examining the accepted practices in our schools. They must rid the schools from the grips of blind tradition and habit, where some are promoted by the sacrifices of others. They must understand that losing more than offsets the benefits of winning, and winning only breeds lust for more until defeat becomes the only possibility.

DOGS AND RATS

Competition is not only fostered in our schools by athletics, high-stakes testing, and grades, but by the way schools attempt to motivate and discipline children. By issuing rewards, singular or collective, environments are created where there is isolation spawned by failure. It occurs when a child faces the rejection alone. However, the roots of competition were spawned during the Industrial Revolution or before, when men began focusing on productivity, using incentives to get more from factory workers. This concept, known as "behaviorism," was applied to the schools, where it was assumed that the same rewards that motivated adults to perform would be effective on children. At the turn of the twentieth century, businessmen became involved to "reshape the schools to fit the new economic social conditions of an urban-industrial society."[19]

Pavlov and Skinner developed theories on classical conditioning (Pavlov's dogs) and operant conditioning (Skinner's rats), which accept the notion of learning and achievement as it relates to the concept of reinforcement as described by Taylor. Skinner applied his work with animals to human behavior and even developed teaching machines where students were conditioned with the correct answer for an immediate "reward." By his own admission, Skinner felt that he had "found a process of conditioning that was different from Pavlov's and much more like learning in daily life."[20] Computer-based, self-instruction uses many of the principles of Skinner's technique. Rewards based on the theories of operant conditioning are nothing more than authoritative control. An idea pioneered by the military and adopted by businesses whose owners were influenced by research on rats and dogs, controlling people like animals is a common acceptance in America's culture that few question anymore. Douglas McGregor's "Theory X" describes the average worker as one who hates work and wants to be controlled. He wants no responsibility and would rather follow than lead.[21] The Theory X model rewards through compensation and competition is based on productivity. Succeeding McGregor at the Massachusetts Institute of Technology was Warren Bennis, whose philosophy contradicts that of his predecessor. He cites Abraham Maslow, who, in *Further Reaches of Human Nature*, states, "Most of us, most of the time listen not to ourselves but, to the voice of the Establishment, of the Elders, of authority, or of tradition."[22] In the case of education, school leadership, or "the Establishment," has adopted the "tradition" established over 100 years ago by behaviorists. Ironically, educators aspire to have children functioning on the highest levels of cognition, which requires critical thinking, the same freedom of thought the establishment intentionally and inadvertently discourages.

Perhaps this mindset has caused recent education reform to be more competitive than ever. Rewards (income), consequences (job security), and competition (blind tradition) are woven into the fabric of modern education. If the end result of competition is extrinsic rewards such as praise, prizes, and recognition, or the lack of them as a consequence of losing, how does the individual ever value intrinsic gratification that leads to self-motivation? To suggest that competition in schools prepares a child for the world of competition is shallow and politically charged. Since we do not have babies compete (I assume I am accurate with this assumption), there has to be a point when adults decide it is time for competitive development. After all, I have not seen office pools where adults place wagers on the date little Junior will walk, or brackets to determine which infants will make it to the final four of breast-feeding. Perhaps Jonathan Kozol whose book *Ordinary Resurrections* features his interactions with success stories that emerge from impoverished schools in the Bronx, attempts to protect childhood development from the clutches of the awaiting adults who think they know best:

> Poor children in America desperately need competitive skills, and realistic recognitions of the economic roles that they may someday have an opportunity to fill are obviously important too. But there is more to life, and ought to be much more to childhood, than readiness for economic function. Childhood ought to have at least a few entitlements that aren't entangled with utilitarian considerations. One of them should be the right to a degree of unencumbered satisfaction in the sheer delight and goodness of existence in itself. Another ought to be the confidence of knowing that one's presence on this earth is taken as an unconditional blessing that is not contaminated by the economic uses that a nation does or does not have for you.[23]

As suggested, all children do not have the same support system at home, which makes competition and the rewards and consequences that go along with it undeniably unfair. It is impossible for researchers to acquire data that would reveal the entire scope of the problem because the trauma causes the children to go into shock mode where they need consoling and support from the child's natural advocate, the parent, who is absent from this process because he/she is usually the abuser. Competition is an enemy to abused and neglected children because it destroys them from the inside out. It does not groom them for adult life, it helps wreck their adult lives. George W. Bush takes care of the top one percent of the nation because they are the leaders of the world order. They are the sponsors of the cause and the power brokers needed for national security. Competition becomes a necessary screening process to prevent nuclear attacks, economic collapses, and any other threat to the United States' position as number one. The abused and neglected are expendable, as are others who fall by the wayside, because they are no threat to national security, or are incapable of preserving it. They become lost, silent, and immeasurable. However, there are those who would prosper in a cooperative environment if they aren't left for dead at such an early age. Some of our greatest leaders have emerged from the trenches of abuse despite the pounding of competitive frustration. Without this constant thrashing, how many more might emerge and find stability, not humility, in school?

Education should internalize the rewards because that is where the battle is being fought. Instead of competitors, the abused needs to feel that others appreciate his contribution to a common good. He does not need to be beaten and defeated by the other child whose family nurtures and supports his or her endeavors. The abused child has learned to internalize and preserve shock because he cannot trust his own family. He carries these burdens with him to school, where his teacher is primarily a judge and his classmates are contestants. He lives in a world, including school, where most are out to beat and control him.

If competition is detrimental to almost all children, it has an increased significance to abused and neglected children. Recommendations for school reform build resiliency in children, something abused children desperately need. Experts agree that there are three characteristics of a resilient child: 1) social competence, 2) problem solving skills, and 3) sense of autonomy.[24,25] Abused children need to feel support in a non-threatening environment to find success. They are not inspired watching others garner rewards and praise while they struggle with shame and low self-esteem. The school that compares children in hierarchical measures is magnifying trauma for the purpose of promoting the elite. Leaders do not seem to care that myths are the excuses driving their lust for competition. Who is going to complain? The abused child, who has internalized the trauma and shock that characterizes his life? His family, which doles out abuse and denial like seconds at Thanksgiving dinner? The teacher, who must objectively control, correct, evaluate, and reward a large number of children on an daily basis? His classmates, competitors who have been pitted against him since preschool? How do consequences for poor behavior, losing, low grades, and watching others receive awards benefit the abused child? Children become nothing more than sacrificial lambs. We condone the practice.

Like child abuse, the adherence to an unquestioned reliance on the powers of competition has become engrained into a vicious cycle that must be broken. Education is not going to be saved by the politicians who are proud to speak for all from perches beyond the classroom, except when posing for publicity photos. Business leaders, who forcibly apply extrinsic motivational practices they feel are successful with adults, don't get it either. These people are products of a flawed system and must remain loyal to that system to sustain their control and power. They are unwilling to learn new things because hiding weaknesses has become more important than growth. Mass production that was made popular at the onset of the industrial age has found its way into our schoolhouses. We made a huge mistake. We have not learned from our history. We cannot extricate our schools from ourselves. We followed the wrong leaders.

BREAKING AWAY

As mentioned, our industrial age's dehumanization for economic and militaristic global competition has had a detrimental impact on modern education. Arguably, the increasing challenges facing education today, single parent families, poverty, declining morality, cyclical abuse patterns, gangs, and many others are, in part, a result of a competitive and elitist school system and a public that no longer questions competition's purpose in our society. The federal and state focus on accountability is legislation that starts in higher government and gives ultimate responsibility to the student-teacher relationship. If education is to ever prosper, the leadership must spawn from the practitioners and the accountability needs to be on the political leaders, both past and current. In essence, educators are currently pressured to appease our elected officials with positive data concerning the accomplishment of minimal standards. Brubaker states:

> Curriculum leaders who are primarily interested in control speak in terms of an efficient educational system. A technically sound system, it is argued, will demonstrate progress in measurable terms. I am amazed and disquieted by the number of superintendents who use the terms *evaluation* and *measurement* synonymously, whereas, in fact, measurement is but one kind of evaluation or assessment. If our

> discussion of the control mode sounds like industrial or factory rhetoric, it is because this language originated in the early years of the Industrial Revolution.[26]

Teachers too have been brainwashed in the competitive model and have been spun dizzy by the fly-by-night, quick fix methods and mandatory testing that taints their trade. State testing is a deterrent to education because it turns children into numbers in their eyes. It tells exam-free teachers that their particular academic disciplines are not worthy of governmental feedback. It places tremendous pressure on those who teach the core subjects that are tested. It suggests that character education, resiliency, socialization, and all other components of healthy child development are trivial matters. In reality, they are the only things that are truly important if education is to be considered in its purest form; it is the state that has emphasized the focus on the regurgitation of trivia and the execution of basic mundane tasks.

The proposal that multitudes of experts have endorsed suggests that true education is exactly the opposite of that into which it has evolved. True education is not measurable; and tests will never reveal anything more than that. It is perhaps a human being's most intrinsic and wholesome activity and is beyond the grasp of legislation. When experts suggest that resiliency is at the core of learning and child development, and cooperative relationships are key protective factors, then competition does not fit into the equation. The current approach is damaging self-esteem and confidence with measurement that is best described as subjective objectivity.

After a child is rejected for inadequacies and easily detectible signs of abuse are ignored, many times that child is shipped to self-contained classrooms for lower performers, simply because the nurturing and support he needs was not provided. I have witnessed an increasing competitive structure in schools that has created a dearth of exceptional children teachers, constant redefining qualifications for special programs, and other measures necessary to maintain a reasonable number of special needs students. Education seems more focused on reinventing curriculum to meet the needs of the state more than attention to learning styles to meet the needs of the children. Numeric characters have become more important than character. Outcome outweighs process, and obedience overshadows discovery. Rhetoric has becomes truth because the search for truth become inconsequential.

The reform ideas that the educational experts, psychologists, philosophers have been screaming for all these years are so simple it would save millions of dollars spent in testing, child protective services, corrections, and many other areas of governmental services that have been established or expanded to sop up the children left behind by current educational practices. Their voices, not backed by major corporations who support political rhetoric in return for the special considerations that have nothing to do with learning, are not heard. Teachers are fed their feel-good, nonsensical messages, but aren't given the necessary training to make it work. In fact, many teachers are verbally abusive and, like the students, may not consider it abuse until they are provided the opportunity to conduct a self-examination. For example, Maxine Greene scholar Jean Anyon describes the failure of teachers to adjust to a particular reform movement that may benefit abused children, insisting on keeping with their techniques that are proven to be detrimental to social and cognitive development. She refers to it as the "abusive school environment."[27] Like their abused students and countless others who have competition's scars on their backs, the teacher refuses to take risks for fear of failure. So she spins protective cocoons and returns to her underachieving areas of comfort and mediocrity.

NOTES

1. Alphie Kohn, *The Schools our Children Deserve: Moving Beyond Traditional Classrooms and "Tougher Standards"* (Boston: Houghton Mifflin, 1999): 3.
2. David Tyack, *The One Best System: A History of American Urban Education* (Cambridge: Harvard UP, 1974): 140.
3. Felecia Romeo,"Child Abuse and Report Cards," *Education*,120, no. 3 (Spring 2000): 438.
4. Romeo, "Child Abuse and Report Cards," 438.
5. Romeo, "Child Abuse and Report Cards," 438.
6. Carol Hanson, "High anxiety," *Teacher Magazine* 10, no. 5 (1999): 36.
7. Peter Senge, *Schools that Learn* (New York: Doubleday, 2000): 49.
8. Senge, *Schools that Learn*, 49.
9. David Purpel, *Moral Outrage in Education* (New York: Peter Lang, 2001): 93.
10. Dale Brubaker, *Creative Curriculum Leadership* (Thousand Oaks, CA: Corwin, 1994): 73.
11. Alfie Kohn, *No Contest: The Case Against Competition* (Boston: Houghton Mifflin, 1986).
12. Andrea Lynn, *Primate Research Says Competition not Driving Force* 2002, <http://unisci.com/stories/20021/0218021.htm> (8 January 2005).
13. Kohn, *No Contest*, 1986.
14. Kohn, *No Contest*, 1986.
15. Kohn, *No Contest*, 1986.
16. Zygmunt Bauman, *Liquid Love* (Cambridge: Polity, 2003): 81.
17. Senge, *Schools that Learn*, 34.
18. James Austin, "Alternatives to Competition in Music Education," *Educational Digest* 55, (1990): 45–49.
19. Tyack, *The One Best System*, 126.

20. B. F. Skinner, *The Shaping of a Behaviorist* (New York: Knopf, 1979): 89.

21. Douglas McGregor, *The Human Side of Enterprise* (New York: McGraw-Hill, 1985).

22. Warren Bennis, *On Becoming a Leader* (New York: Basic Books, 2003): 105.

23. Jonathan Kozol, *Ordinary Resurrections* (New York: Perennial, 2000): 141–142.

24. Bonnie Benard, "Fostering Resiliency in Kids," *Educational Leadership* 67, (2001): 44–48.

25. Marty Krovetz, "Resiliency: A Key Element for Supporting Youth At-risk," *The Clearing House* 73, no. 2, (1999): 121–124.

26. Brubaker, *Creative Curriculum Leadership,* 13.

27. William Ayers and Janet Miller eds., *A Light in Dark Times: Maxine Greene and the Unfinished Conversation* (New York: Teacher's College, Columbia UP, 1998).

Chapter Six

The Resilient Self

"Knowledge emerges only through invention and re-invention, through the restless, impatient, continuing, hopeful inquiry human beings pursue in the world, with the world, and with each other."

—Paulo Freire, *Pedagogy of the Oppressed*

A SWEATY NOTE

Mr. Michael was one of my eleventh grade teachers who claimed to have UFO's hovering over his house from time to time. If superior life forms actually were orbiting his dwelling, they were probably only attempting to get a snapshot or two of him to validate their stories back on their home planet. Retrospectively, he reminds me of Doc, Christopher Lloyd's character in the *Back to the Future* trilogy, possessing the same passion for his particular science, American literature. Every day he wore one of four leisure suits, the cornerstones of his outdated and rather unimpressive wardrobe. The color sequence never altered, blue, brown, green, and tan, and then back to the blue. The silky screened shirts he wore beneath were loud and rather humorous, featuring multi-colored clowns, tropical fish, or classic automobiles, among others. Regardless of the outfit, he wore suede Wallabies, tan Hushpuppy high tops with leather laces and a yellowish, semi-transparent, spongy sole that squeaked on the institutional tile in his classroom. When he talked his hair stayed in place, but when he taught, when the spirit of literature overcame him, his silver comb-over would fall into his reddened face, usually dampened by perspiration. Sometimes strands would adhere to the corners of his eyes, something that never seemed to bother him. He had two voices.

When he was calm, he sounded like Marlon Brando's *Godfather* character, with the same raspy quality but with a Southern accent. But when he felt the spirit of his lesson, when the ghosts of our nation's top scribes took over his body, he became, well, Christopher Lloyd.

Mr. Michael, like the movie character, was also a time traveler of sorts. After all, it was he who introduced me to a couple of men he called his "oldest hippy friends," Ralph Waldo Emerson and Henry David Thoreau. He taught their transcendental wisdom with the same vigor of a fly-by-night pastor saving souls at tent revivals across the deep South. To me it was miraculous and more than therapeutic; it began the dismantling of my internal prison. Emerson and Thoreau's inspiring philosophy calmed the rage and panic within me like cool waters flowing across reddened embers. Transcendentalism became a romantic reality to me, a state of mind that encouraged individuality and an awareness that all things are connected by God and to God. It legitimized my purpose as an insecure boy who was still trying to stand while it seemed others were dancing. The message had special significances for every child in the classroom, even those with happy homes who had reason to be confident and secure. Of course, being a child is difficult enough and many of the challenges facing one, face all. But for an abused and insecure boy of sixteen, Mr. Michael's literary resurrections helped exorcise the demons inside that were feeding on my life's potential.

Through Mr. Michael's love for his subject and his students, the connectedness between the figurative ideal and the actual circumstances of my life personalized the hope I felt belonged exclusively to others. He gave me the wisdom of these great thinkers, and, in a matter of a few days, I owned their words. I felt that they left the key to my freedom behind in a capsule for me alone to pry open while sitting on the front row in his eleventh grade English class. Ralph and Henry may have taught me "insist on yourself, never imitate," and warned that "the mass of men lead lives of quiet desperation," but Mr. Michael gave me the courage to act on it. Classroom discussions where we laughed and discussed literary content, with the same comfort we might have talked about a ball game or a television show, were very common. We all shared personal opinions and facts about ourselves, but there was one aspect of my life I always left alone.

Mr. Michael must have known that I was at the crossroads, and if I chose the path of others in this particular school, I might follow them carelessly toward my own tragic demise. I would be condemned to a life of "quiet desperation," beating my children and calling them the same names that I was called, made true by the inability to navigate my own course. There must be something sadly tragic when one realizes that his life is at its end and awakens to the awareness that he chose a barren street to travel from adolescence until remorse and regret have carved every contour into a wrinkled and dejected face. I refused that existence. Mr. Michael had mastered his hidden curriculum and he lived it beautifully. He knew his students. He spoke to me and to my situation, and it comforted me to know that I must be a nonconformist because that is how I would save myself. If anything, Mr. Michael showed me that it is acceptable to be different and there is providence in breaking away from the norm, discovering your self, and then becoming just that. More significantly, life has no meaning until you start living your own life, but to do that, you have to listen to what your self is telling you to do. Perhaps I was not crazy to listen when my inner child spoke. It seems to have worked for Mr. Michael, but then again, he seemed to hear lots of voices.

Emerson was the one of the pair with whom I connected. Thoreau was articulate and philosophical, but he followed Emerson; I chose to be guided by a pioneer, not a settler. I never understood why Thoreau wasted his Harvard education sweeping porches and living beside a pond. He was nothing but potential and excuses but his poetic words resonated in me. I remember Mr. Michael jokingly blurting comments about Thoreau's departure from the pond when we read *Walden* aloud, "Right! Have you ever lived through a Massachusetts winter with no heat? He got the heck out there when those winds started blowing off of that pond and snapping at his nose!" We laughed as if he was referring to a comical character, one that we could all could relate to because we met him together. Mr. Michael helped us forge relationships with the writers through analysis, cooperative activities, explication, and a humor only he could deliver. It was okay to laugh at him, Thoreau, the Puritans (he had a ball with them), Ben Franklin—and in the process, we learned to laugh at ourselves. It was Emerson who spoke to me because Mr. Michael, in his indirect style, made sure that I was familiar with two quotes. The first, he had me read aloud in class, occasionally stopping me and discussing it so vividly that he unintentionally brought tears to my eyes. He handed me the second on a piece of notebook paper marked by frantic handwriting, as if he was afraid it would vanish before capturing it.

Reading excerpts from "Self-Reliance" aloud was the most powerful intervention I have ever experienced. I thought that my family life was a secret. I knew that my brother's antics were making him a household name around town, but I had no idea this crazy, polyester-suit-wearing, time-traveling, friend of E.T. had any clue about my disposition. My pain was internal and my mask had no cracks. As children, before we knew what the word "invisible" meant, my siblings and I would dream that adults "couldn't hardly see" us. We imagined the feeling of emancipation as we slid by grown ups without fear of being hit or verbal condemnation. Since then that is exactly what I had done. My behavior was acceptable, but not because I had goals; it was motivated by fear, a lack of confidence, and a strong desire to be left alone. So I had been invisible for the longest time before Mr. Michael's class, but if he could see aliens and the subtle nonconformity of donning leisure suits in public, he would see me. The passages he placed beneath my nose gave me validity and showed that he, not men who had been dead for nearly a century, might have understood me. He must have seen that "something" behind my eyes. He must have been abused himself and perhaps he was called into teaching to end his role in his own vicious cycle. I will never know.

"Gerry, why don't you read the next passage?" That itself was a signal that he was on to me because Mr. Michael always asked volunteers to read and never called on someone who didn't have a raised hand. He would explain that reading is a personal thing and it embarrasses some people to read aloud because they read slower, have speech impediments, mispronounce words, and so on. His aim was to promote desire, not extinguish it. I obliged, reading some stuff I couldn't interpret because the vocabulary was difficult and the language ornate, but after Mr. Michael's explanation, the passage that he stopped class to discuss possibly had personal significance. I read Emerson's words that state, "It is easy in the world to live after the world's opinion; it is easy in solitude to live after our own; but the great man is he who in the midst of the crowd keeps with perfect sweetness the independence of solitude." After thinking it through, a process that blurred my comprehension even more, I wasn't exactly sure what it meant if it were actually meant for me in particular. Was it a compliment, advice, or a warning? I felt as if the words were rather ambiguous, but he stirred in me a fear that my invisibility was wearing off. I felt that it was telling me to be myself in public, not just in my own little world. I took my textbook home and ventured into my lair and re-read "Self-Reliance" until I was so confused and the words became so abstract that I couldn't comprehend the simplest logic. Mr. Michaels knew that Emerson's "trust thyself" theme would rock my world. In less than forty-eight hours, it would be rocked again.

Two days later, Mr. Michael was concluding our unit on American Romanticism and I had resumed the normalcy of my dual existence. Again, his clothes would have been humorous had we not grown accustomed to them by that time, and we might have thrown a cruel verbal zinger his way had we all not been so fond of him. Even though nobody with a job had worn leisure suits in nearly a decade, it was never fashionable to wear a polyester shirt that featured black and white penguins against a white and blue oceanic background with a chocolate-brown suit. Because he was so symbolic and interesting, every faux pas and every eccentric act was interpreted to have some link to the text and to our worlds in general. "The brown reflects pollution that is spreading to the purest regions on earth, so our next unit will focus on corruption and the frigid nature of human formality," we might have humorously hypothesized if we had only been smarter. I don't think he was testing us, but we thirsted for meaning in every aspect of our time with him. And we found it.

During his closing remarks, he fabricated a conversation between Emerson, Thoreau, and himself by jumping from spot to spot on the floor, whimsically and spontaneously switching in and out of character while creating a dialogue using some of the quotes we had discussed. It was not only a terrific review, but also a classic piece of improvisational comedy. His hair dropped into his red face and his bald spot shimmering through the remaining silver strands; he paused for the laughter to cease in order to properly present his next side-splitting line. You could tell by his smug, impatient grin that he was a few hilarious puns ahead of us, but he panted patiently until the laughter waned. He didn't mind being our stooge if we were learning. Of course, I saw not a lunatic or dolt at the front of the class. I saw a genius who knew children and refused to abandon his childhood because it was the vessel with which he connected to us. We had to know our material to understand his satire. Knowing the text was a side effect of the class, the tool we used to explore through interaction. He was a man whose classroom was more about us than the subject. Retrospectively, that is all that I was looking for. That is all my classmates were looking for, abused or not. And that is what we found.

I was sure the laughter booming from our room was disturbing the other classes, and knew that my friends, yawning through the lectures of other teachers just down the hall, would be envious of our experience. All he had were the antiquated words of dead men, but he slapped us alive with the beauty of their minds in a manner we could have never seen without him. Mr. Michael was more than a good teacher for me and others who had insecurities of their own, he was a savior who rose from the debris of the public school system. He saw how literature had the power to ease pain and boost self-esteem. He sold it to us because he had already bought into it himself. Although he would give us one the following day, he said we didn't need a test, and he was painfully correct. Our test would be how well we would apply his gift to our lives, how well we utilized the resiliency he nurtured. He found his feedback in our eyes, our laughter, and our attention to every word. A grade would actually be rather insignificant and insulting.

When the bell rang, I remember feeling a little disappointment (as I had in the past), which was odd because in most schools the passing of time is the only thing celebrated. As I stacked my books on the desktop to begin my march down the hall toward Algebra II, he passively approached me, perhaps fearful that he might offend. He dropped the torn piece of notebook paper with the scribbled quote into my hand. It was moist with perspiration, as if he had been holding it throughout his impersonations. "You can throw it away if you don't find meaning in it," he said and returned to his desk. His honest face, still marked with the lines of laughter and speckled with droplets of perspiration, was suddenly somber and concerned. He dropped his gaze into a book as if to silently suggest that I read the note carefully, something that was already a given. Intrigued and embarrassed by the attention, I stuffed it into my pocket because I sensed that he didn't want me to read it in his presence, grabbed my books, and headed out into the crowded hallway.

Before math class the mystery in my pocket quickly overcame me, but I waited until the tardy bell rang before reading it because opportunities for social interaction were kept at a minimum in a rough high school like the one I attended. Except for the discussions in Mr. Michael's class, it was the only opportunity for students to communicate with one another without getting into trouble. The paper was soft from the moisture, so it didn't make the usual crinkling sound as I retrieved it during the math teacher's droning, and the blue ink was bleeding in places, but not as much as to make it illegible. The words I then read initially stunned me, perhaps angered me, as if my privacy had been violated. But my favorite teacher carefully selected them and these particular words were written a century ago, so there was just cause to reel myself back in and consider these initial feelings to be nothing more than one of my classic and customary overreactions. I knew this was his effort to help, so I accepted the note in the spirit in which it was offered. In the words of Emerson but in the hand of Mr. Michael, the scribbled quote read, "A low self-love in the parent desires that his child should repeat his character and fortune."

I couldn't breathe for a moment. He was asking me to start breaking the cycle, to rid myself of the trappings that have stigmatized my parents and free myself from their destinies. He knew my problem was with my parents before I came to terms with it. I didn't know how to react, but it was delightful and equally horrifying to know that a man I respected, a man who seemed to be nothing more than a visitor on this planet, could have the insight to recognize the subtleties I thought were so well hidden. This man, who knew that wisdom and courage are partners, had the intelligence and the guts to see inside me and reach out to help. It gave me validity, an understanding that the frustrations of my parents are what actually inspired their blind cruelty. Most importantly, someone could see it, and knew that I was not totally to blame for my low self-esteem and distorted reality. I flashed back to another quote from his role-playing finale that might have been for my benefit, but I couldn't have known it at the time. During his three-way conversation that had us laughing hysterically was another Emersonian phrase that I would later embrace: "My giant goes with me wherever I go."

"What is my giant?" I wondered. Later, I would eventually discuss aspects of my home life with Mr. Michael, and he would listen. He usually responded by recalling quotations from other writers, some of which have escaped my memory, but some did not. He didn't judge or pity; he refused to allow excuses. He gave me resiliency, which meant that his teaching would impact the rest of my life.

During my high school experience, I had approximately 35 different teachers and spent over 170 hours with each. Only one had the courage and insight to reach me, and it has made all the difference to me. Before that, in elementary school, I remember frequently going to school with bluish-red belt whelps on my legs and back, finding walking difficult at times. I spent an approximate 12,000 hours under the watchful eyes of school personnel and not one recognized the problem, or worse, some must have chosen to ignore it. It took over ten years, but finally one noticed, using his academic discipline like a surgeon's scalpel, removing the calcified tissue and infection that a decade of abuse creates. I had only been in his class for about three months, roughly 60 hours, for him to spot me and reach out. And there were no fresh wounds to see; the beatings had ceased by then because my family was rapidly dissolving and I had outgrown that brand of abuse.

I do not blame the other teachers for not recognizing the situation because abuse had never been an area of child development that administration has deemed worthy of teacher training. I do, however, owe more than I will ever be able to repay to one man who showed me how to turn scars into character and setbacks into motivation. At no point did he ever assume the posture of hovering over me like his green friends; instead, he walked with me and changed my life. Jesus, Gandhi, and Martin Luther King Jr. are revered because they were able to see suffering and willing to make the ultimate sacrifices to end it. If students witness adults who care enough to take chances, then they will have the model they need to release the grip on their insecurities and take the risks that will give their education meaning. This is not measured by darkening little bubbles with a number two pencil.

Three years later I became an English major in college. I recognize characteristics in strangers and compare them to pilgrims in *The Canterbury Tales,* which helps me analyze people more quickly. Few understood the human condition and the repetitious design of man and how well it transcends time better than Geoffrey Chaucer. I analyzed the significance of my father's death through Shakespeare's *Hamlet,* where Hamlet, Laertes, and young Fortinbras all lose fathers prematurely. *Romeo and Juliet* taught me the danger of youth without patience. I wept for the orphaned children who died young sweeping London chimneys in the late eighteenth century poetry of William Blake. Homer metaphorically showed me the temptations and challenges in life and taught me that the journey and the decisions one makes along the way, not the destination, is the actual meaning of life. He told me to avoid the Sirens (temptations), the lotus (drugs and alcohol), and that sometimes you find yourself in a position where there is no easy way out, but a wise captain chooses the better way (Scylia and Charybdis). My Odyssey will have no grand finale; only the footprints that I left, or failed to leave behind, will be significant. There are few situations one can face that that haven't already been presented to me in literature. But most of all, Mr. Michael showed me how to be myself and to listen to that little voice that guides me through the chaos of my world. He gave me back to my rightful owner. He showed me a philosophy that gave my life meaning, even if it misguided me at times. Maturity would help me regulate this power and selectively use it moderately. Regardless, it became purpose and courage.

HOT WATER

The summer after Mr. Michael's class ended, I accepted a lucrative position in the poultry industry. I had never worked third shift before, but since I would avoid the drama at home by sleeping when everyone else was awake, I liked it. My job varied, but primarily I ran a high-powered hose that shot a fervent stream of steaming hot water into processing machines in an assembly line, ridding them of dislodged feathers and feet that had broken off during the chickens' futile struggle for life. Many of my esteemed colleagues were proud participants in the local medium-security prison's fabled work-release program. This added to the already significant pressure and stress that was attributed to a man in my position because the tiny corridors that housed the assembly machinery would get very steamy and hot. That steam made it difficult to see coworkers, and there were times the high-pressured hose would coil loose from my grip, swerving and weaving its nose like a threatening cobra. These were the moments I saw a direct correlation between heat and anger. I specifically learned this when I inadvertently scalded the face of the inmate they called "Streak" with a bolt of water jetting out of my hose at about 50 miles per hour and at a temperature of 130 degrees. The hot fog was thick and Streak was supposed to watch for me instead of the other way around, but somehow he seemed to forget that segment of the ninety-second training film. Even though he was about 6 feet and 5 inches tall and weighed nearly 300 pounds, my vision was very limited and I did not see him. I didn't realize that I had angered the incarcerated behemoth until I heard the scream and profanity that immediately followed. This worst-case scenario was confirmed when I saw the shadowy image of his baseball cap flipping away from his head into the mist of the moment, as I stepped from inside that tunneled machine out into the folklore of local the prison yard.

Perhaps this isn't the best time to interrupt the events being described to give Streak a little more character development, but I had recently learned from his buddies that he was a feared man in prison because he had a bad temper. He had been in prison for several years for cutting a man open when he found him with his woman, and then stabbing each of her breasts. The upper management in this particular processing plant decided that Streak should be given a ten-inch knife with a razor sharp edge and assign him the task of cutting chicken feet from hangers because, I assumed, such a job was his only marketable skill.

At any rate, he became less foggy and more defined as he stomped toward me with the knife in hand, still cursing profusely. "Drop that damn hose, boy!" As much as I wanted to cooperate with him to help decrease his level of anxiety, I wasn't dropping the damn hose. I held it firmly, pointing its bolt of steaming water downward intro a drain designed for chicken blood. I didn't see that particular irony at the time. Again, and slower, he repeated, "I said, drop the damn hose, boy!"

If he thought the water was warm and aggravating twenty feet away, I had to consider that it would be a rather suitable weapon at five feet. "Take another step and you will get another mouthful!" I bluffed. He took another step. There was an increasing congregation of inmates surrounding me, seemingly not too interested in helping me out. It occurred to me that they were all afraid of him, trying to win his favor by encouraging him to use the knife on me. It was then I would have liked for one of Mr. Michael's aliens to swoop down and abduct me, but the stench of the plant even kept dogs away, so beings of superior intelligence were nowhere in my immediate vicinity. He stepped again, and I could see the veins pulsing at his temples and the way in which he was holding the knife. I took comfort in the fact that he was gripping it to slice me, with his index finger running up the spine of the blade, which was better than the "stabbing me" variety. That was something I learned in high school. I also knew that he was in a difficult social position; he'd lose all of his hard-earned respect if he backed down. Then I concluded that the witnesses would all say that I started the ordeal by intentionally washing his face from across the corridor, causing Streak to act in self-defense. I also realized that his next step would put me within an arm's reach, and I wasn't going to back up, showing him any more fear than he already sensed; I learned to stand my ground in high school and it seemed to serve me well. These thoughts raced through my head in a second or two, and none were very comforting. He stared at me, and I stared back. His lips were wet and trembling beneath his anxious, bloodshot eyes. Why I chose that moment to reflect on Mr. Michael's class, specifically the wisdom of Ralph Waldo Emerson, shows the power of literature and good teaching. "Trust thyself," I thought, "Whoso would be a man, must be a nonconformist." I was certain that Streak was accustomed to fearful men, sacrificing dignity in order to live to see their paroles. Had he ever been challenged? Would he know what to do? I didn't really want to discover the answer, but I was betting that he had never been face-to-face in a confrontation with a boy, barely seventeen, who wasn't even flinching. Perhaps the fact that I was being brash was a stroke of brilliance. Emerson whispered again, "My giant goes with me wherever I go." I decided that my giant was courage.

I had to yell because it was a noisy place, "If I have to throw a couple gallons of this water up your nose, I won't think twice. . ." the water lost pressure. One of his prison buddies turned off the valve on the wall behind me and the stream gradually arched downward and drooped into a trickle. I stared down at my unfortunate drought as if the last moments of my life were sliding down the drain, where my blood would be blending with that of a thousand fryers. Everybody, including Streak, mercilessly laughed as the power dripped from my only weapon. He looked at me and stopped laughing, but could not maintain a straight face. I maintained eye contact, but failed to see humor in any aspect of the last forty seconds. "Ah-ite den." He said to me, then turned and walked away. The others followed, many of them looking back and telling me that I was "a lucky-ass white boy," and that he would eventually get me. I stared at them too, probably because it had proven to be successful and I didn't have any interest in stirring any of them up with another dash of my Clint Eastwood-style bravado. I quickly revitalized my hose, crawled back into my processing machine where I sat motionless amidst the rows of rubber de-feathering fingers, letting the adrenaline run its course through my veins until the dizziness and shaking ceased.

The following night, Streak plopped down beside me with his dinner in the break room. He looked at me and laughed. "Boy, you wuz lucky I ain't lookin' to git in no mo' trouble. I wuz gonna cut yo' ass sho' nuff."

"No you weren't." I replied calmly, convinced that I backed him down the prior evening by not backing down to him. If you would have come another step closer, I was going up your nose with it."

He laughed. "I knowed you would. I could tell dat you would," he laughed again, before looking at me seriously. "You woulda made a mistake," he mumbled with a mouthful of sandwich.

"I didn't have too many choices. If I used the hose, you would have eventually cut me. You had to. You got a rep. If I dropped the hose, you still would have had to do something to get me back."

"Now dat's how it works. But it wuz funny as hell when dat water dropped off an' you coulda seen yo' face!"

"Why didn't you cut me then?"

"I told you, I ain't wanna do no mo' time."

I knew what he meant. The loss of pressure was funny to everyone except me, but more importantly, it gave him an out. Although Mr. Michael's alien brethren never rescued me, I was visited by one of his hippy friends from the grave, whose advice showed me that confidence and knowledge are tools that I can use to avoid conflict, even when it seems inevitable. By standing up to Streak, I spent the rest of my summer as a respected co-worker, an honorary member of the North Carolina Department of Corrections' work-release program. Because I had personalized the lessons I explored in English class, my life had already changed, and I was applying my learning to adverse situations in the world beyond the walls of school. I realize that my possible misinterpretation of Emerson's meaning could have been painful, but the point is, I fused my education with my judgment and utilized them in a stressful situation. I had internalized English literature. I was using it to solve problems. I was becoming resilient.

MASTER OF MY FATE

When I look back at Mr. Michael's class, it is interesting that I would convert the teachings of a nerdy, eccentric English teacher into a stressful situation far removed from the academic arena. The significance does not lie in the retrieval of quotations or Ralph Waldo Emerson's pre-bout wisdom. There was something more important at work, something I only recently acknowledged while reading about resiliency in an effort to understand why I took the path that was not traversed by my brother and sister. I stepped beyond the fear and intimidation that had been synonymous with my existence. It even seemed to catch Streak, the most revered inmate from the local prison, momentarily off guard. His reasons for backing off are not clear or important. The fact that my mind took me to a place where I felt empowered is significant because I, not the large and overbearing adult, was able to control the situation, at least to a degree. I used knowledge and experience obtained in an effective classroom to overcome a major obstacle, even though fear dominated my mind. I looked him directly in the eye and was willing to face the challenge should that have been necessary, and the challenge was one of infinite possibilities for failure. I was afraid but not vulnerable, both before and after the water was shut off. I knew the long-term consequences of retreat and, whether it was smart or not, chose to face the problem. I was trembling and very tired because I was not used to sleeping days, but I met the man I was to become that night and liked him. It was the self that was to become in charge of my destiny, the self that refused to allow me to be helplessly victimized any longer. I do not know why I chose to prove this in an adversarial confrontation with such an imposing man. That had less to do with resiliency than the stupidity of a teenager. Nonetheless, when one overcomes obstacles like Streak, the mountains begin to look climbable, the night is never again as dark, and the demons that deform lives start heading for the exits.

"Promotion of resiliency lies in encountering stress at a time and in a way that allows a person to experience mastery and appropriate responsibility, thus increasing his or her sense of self-confidence and competence."[1] Resilient people cope with stress better because they are able to confidently select from various acquired skills and abilities in stressful situations. I didn't have an arsenal of these acquired skills and abilities at the time of my encounter with Streak, but for the first time my life featured an adult who believed in me, and that gave me the courage to stand my ground against a huge, rather annoyed, prison inmate with a ten-inch blade standing only two paces away. "Children have an intrinsic need for mastery over situations, a need that they express by using their experiences to search out significant patterns in reality and thus reduce uncertainty."[2] Although I thought that I might be killed or severely injured and would be washed down the drain with the rest of the remnants, at least my guts would unmistakably not be those of a chicken—an idiot, perhaps, but not a chicken.

"The hallmarks of a resilient child include knowing how to solve problems or knowing that there's an adult to turn to for help," explains Robert Brooks, a clinical psychologist on the faculty of Harvard Medical School. "A resilient child has some sense of mastery of his own life, and if he gets frustrated by a mistake, he still feels he can learn from the mistake."[3] Although there are many rather similar definitions of resiliency, Richardson describes it as a process by which "people have the opportunity to grow from the adversity and challenges of life by strengthening protective factors and developing a healthy integration of mind, body, and spirit."[4] It is these protective factors that are of concern to educators who would like to see abused and neglected children become contributing members of the student body, colleges, and eventually, the community. Without protective factors, children are at risk of becoming disciplinary problems, dropouts, and then prison inmates like Streak. The implementation of these factors leads to the skills and abilities listed in a 1987 article featured in *Child Abuse and Neglect*:

1. Rapid response to danger: The ability to recognize and adapt to the requirements of an immediate social setting in order to avoid harm.
2. Precocious maturity/pseudoadulthood: The child engages in role reversal, usually with his or her parents.

3. Disassociation of affect: The ability to distance oneself from intense feelings.
4. Information seeking: The desire to learn as much as possible about hazards in the environment.
5. Formation and utilization of relationships for survival: The ability to create relationships that result in critical help or support in times of crisis.
6. Positive projective anticipation: The ability to project oneself into the future and to fantasize about how life will be when the difficult times are over.
7. Decisive risk-taking: The ability to assume personal responsibility by making some crucial decision even if the decision carries some personal risk.
8. The conviction of being loved: The ability to believe that one deserves to be loved.
9. Idealization of aggressor's competence: The ability to identify with some aspect of the aggressor's competence.
10. Cognitive restructuring of painful events: The ability to reprocess negative events in a way that will make them more acceptable or congruent with one's view.
11. Altruism: The ability to gain pleasure from giving to others.
12. Optimism and hope: the disposition to take a positive view of events that will happen in the future.[5]

It seems that this list begins with the simpler, more concrete application of resilience and elevates to the more complex and abstract mastery. Although the source did not specifically call it a hierarchy, it seems to rise from coping to intrinsic, positive adjustments. Many of the things listed are the by-products of Mr. Michael's classroom. The misunderstanding with Streak exemplified my clumsy attempt to apply this learned resiliency to a stressful situation. At that time however, I am not sure that development had begun in a few of the later abilities listed.

In four studies conducted by education professors from California, Colorado, and Norway, respectively, researchers compared students' levels of resiliency with academic performance. They arrived at the following conclusions after developing a resiliency scale by which to measure the level of resiliency in relation to academic success:

> Persons scoring higher on the resiliency scale are likely to demonstrate better academic skills; have a higher internal locus of control orientation, have higher self-perceived competence in scholastics, jobs, athletic performance, and friendships; and display a wider range of coping skills than less resilient peers. Depressed resiliency scores may be associated with the occurrence of traumatic

> events in the adolescents' lives. This suggests that resilient individuals endorse a different set of beliefs that enable them to acquire and use more effective coping skills in times of stress.[6]

These results are extremely significant because, not shockingly, they prove a direct link between the level of resiliency and academic performance and other forms of success. It reveals a scale by which resiliency can be identified, monitored, and measured, which might help the politicians comprehend its importance. Since resiliency is important and there are varying degrees of severity that inflict our children, why are we teaching to a test? Why are we taking tests?

Therefore, teachers, parents, and schools must focus on the long-term ideals that will not coincide with presidential, gubernatorial, or school board elections. They must develop and maintain the aforementioned protective factors; this won't be done with grant money, cosmetic curricular changes, or the mandate of a policy. It is definitely not the product of student competition, high-stakes testing, elitist programs, or elaborate awards ceremonies. It will not evolve from quantitative studies or feasibility plans. It comes from the heart, the immeasurable capacity for adults and children to cooperate in a caring, nurturing place. If we build the protective factors in all children, not just those who suffer from the sickness of child abuse, test scores will improve across the board. However, they should not improve as a goal, but as a secondary reaction to good teaching. The thrills of exploration and discovery have no gold, silver, bronze, or participation recognitions. They are unique to each student and compare to nothing else. "People with a high sense of self-efficacy are likely to approach achievement situations with confidence and engage in tasks willingly and persistently."[7]

Learning is an innate, natural process that is a reward in itself and is going to occur regardless of schools, parental support, and adult supervision. It is the confidence and the network of resources that must be defined and improved by the adults who are the guardians of youth in the school and community. A child does not grow by surpassing another child, and the child who is defeated definitely does not learn to value the experience of being labeled inferior, regardless of the intent to build character through competition. By refining strengths children are empowered to seek new challenges and become strong in other areas. This does not happen when the child retreats to a world darkened by the shadows that the competitive sun creates. A good farmer knows that he must tend to his entire crop to be successful. A rancher's concern is the herd as a whole. Both nurture, feed, and satisfy needs to succeed. No competition.

BOTTOM UP

Recognizing the signs of abuse and neglect and knowing how to address the problem is paramount in determining the possible need for outside resources, individual attention, and peer acknowledgement. It does not suggest that resiliency development is solely for abused kids. "All students can overcome adversity if important protective factors are present in their lives."[8] Resiliency is basically the overcoming of obstacles and the growth that occurs from the utilization of intrinsic and extrinsic resources that contribute to the completion of the task. How is that different from the development of higher-order cognitions and advancements in the affective domain? Are they not one in the same, or at least first cousins? The rub, therefore, lies in the manner in which public schools do their part in establishing an environment where students become resilient utilizing the highest levels of thinking. For the well-adjusted, upper-echelon students, the structure needs overhauling in some areas and tweaking in others. For the groundlings in the schools, as is the case with abused and neglected children, there must be a process of rebuilding that starts within the child. The fears and insecurities must gradually be eliminated, which may be difficult as the student is passed from grade to grade, where they tend to get lost. We have folders that follow them, but all teachers do not read them at the beginning of the year and they are of limited value. Even when teachers do scan the folders, many are looking for grades, negative reports, and test scores, which means nothing more than our intervention would be skewed from the start.

Schools, therefore, by the construct based on Pavlovian dogs and Skinnerian rats and the lessons of the Industrial Revolution and the dehumanizing logic of Charles Darwin that we stopped questioning years ago, do little to foster resiliency. We pack small children into large classrooms. Some teachers' class loads are so immense that they hardly bother trying to learn all of the names of the children. The students with gifted abilities and those who become infamous behavior problems become known, but others remain anonymous. The school is a place where bells trigger cattle drives to the next class; I have observed teachers blowing whistles in the hallways like concerned lifeguards. Students get inferior grades slapped on their desks by over-worked, under-paid teachers and must endure the smugness of brighter kids waving their papers around like Pittsburgh Steeler fans with their "terrible towels." We cut kids from the basketball team because they are not good enough, or because their fathers were not around to sway the coach's opinion. Some teachers find programs such as cooperative learning and other forms of differentiated instruction to be impractical because they do not want relinquish control.

Australian researchers suggest that the same problems facing teachers here are facing them down under:

> Anecdotal evidence suggests that many teachers find their energies concentrated on maintaining order and discipline in classrooms at the expense of teaching. Others believe that some children's social and emotional needs are so great that the bulk of their effort must be directed towards this 'welfare work'. If a focus on achievement, competence, and skill development has dropped in the list of some schools' priorities, it is all too understandable.[9]

It is not surprising that the school curriculum, established on the assumption that pitting students against one another to determine recipients of high marks and awards, would have a high concentration of delinquency problems and "welfare work." Many students, including abused and neglected children, are not having their needs met. Add to the equation tremendous class sizes and other problems beyond a teacher's control, and the appropriate question would be, "What did you expect?"

Students having to endure teacher-centered, whole-class instruction get bored. When a child whose needs are not being met loses interest, it is a matter of time before discipline problems, withdrawal, or other forms of rebellion occur. When twenty or thirty children lose interest, the teacher transforms from educator into referee. *The majority of classroom disciplinary problems could be eliminated by deleting nearly all forms of competition and utilizing techniques that have been proven protectors in the establishment of resiliency.* The teacher's role diminishes to that of a facilitator more often than lecturer. The focus is not on teaching, but supporting the process of learning by instilling the confidence in children to take risks and tackle problems. Some teachers do not understand that teaching occurs only when there is learning. This is achieved by providing the proper stimuli, not by giving out the most information. Learning is intrinsic and must have value to the learner, not the teacher. Teachers must create stimulating environments that encourage discovery, not rob them of the experience by condensed trivia or data. Teachers and administrators need to forget about test scores; they are too one-dimensional and measure minimal standards. A child who scores a few questions above random chance on state tests is considered proficient. It is a negative approach to education and those responsible for testing ought to be extricated from their positions of leadership. If the teachers and administrators would release the leash and let the kids explore on their own, the return would exceed test score minimums and save a large group of children mired in the mud of abuse and neglect. Some students consider themselves poor test takers. By promoting the test all year and stressing the significance of passing, teachers are putting undue pressure on students. Some will crumble because they are not confident. Abused and neglected children are highly at risk for failure for this reason. Remembering that minimally around 10 percent or more of all children are abused and/or neglected, and there are many more who will succumb to this mounting stress, the "high-pressure sales" technique is more likely to have a negative impact on test scores than not.

Successful educational reform must start with the students-teacher relationships and end with the governor or president, not otherwise, which has been the process that brings us to where we are. We are constantly trying to correct the problems on a sinking ship by constantly changing the sails. However, reform that begins in the school *has* been successful. Ontario developed a vision at the top and allowed for a "bottom-up" reform movement. That vision epitomizes the most wholesome and productive qualities of education, as expressed by an Ontario educational leader:

> We have a strong belief that, in order for children to really understand the basics, they have to have a problem-solving ability of their own. So we encourage creative thinking and critical thinking, and we provide all sorts of opportunities for kids to write and speak with their teachers and with their peers, to come to grips with their own understanding of things. It isn't just a matter of taking it in and spitting it out. We continue to emphasize basics. What is different is that, rather than getting *back* to basics, we think we are getting *forward* to basics. That means that rather than returning to the traditional rote teaching methods, and all the achievement testing that goes along with that, we look forward to more creative teaching methods, based on a student's experience, and helping students create meaning out of their lives.[10]

This describes the environment that nurtures abused and neglected children, because it gives all children the opportunity to "create meaning out of their lives." They are not expected to fit a mold or meet degrading minimal standards, they are pushed to excel and explore their worlds in a cooperative, caring environment free from competition and extrinsic rewards. When compared to the statement of a political leader who claims to have been the "education governor," the differences in the visions are astounding.

Former North Carolina Governor Jim Hunt shows this lack of understanding in his book, *First in America,* a rather self-promoting, competitive title that properly reflects the theme of its contents, even though the title is only the actual truth if fragmented, distorted, and selective data is considered to embody trace amounts of realism. He provides the law-abiding, tax-paying, and voting citizens with inspirational quotes such as, "That is where we came up with the idea of an annual report card to show who number one is: what is best, and who is best."[11] "The stakes are high. What we need is full accountability."[12] We as a society failed them (under-performing students and drop outs). We didn't measure and report."[13] Although one should appreciate his intentions and realize that Mr. Hunt is simply a product of the competitive system that empowered him, he illustrates the problem with top-down educational reform and a political determination of how it should occur.

Education must first be a matter of personal security before it becomes a matter of national security. However, it seems obvious that the economic and military advisors, not those involved in education, have had the most influence on our leaders in stirring changes in public school curriculum. It is hard to rationalize why politics and education became so entwined, but few would argue that the most dynamic events in American history have coincided with the most drastic reform movements in education. It is my contention that these quick fix, panicked approaches to reform by non-qualified governmental employees have severely stunted educational progress. And these are the leaders who want accountability and measurement. The Industrial Revolution, world wars, Sputnik, the cold war, The civil rights movement, Japan's economic invasion, and other events that caused our government to fear the future, spawned change more than any amount or educational, psychological, or social research. How can education be beneficial to the whole child if it is a product of fear?

The current, globally-competitive model eliminates the encouragement and growth of students labeled "at-risk" through a blind system of humiliation, consequences, and measurement. If we have to play the politician's game, then begin the reform effort on the grass roots level. Manipulate their doctrines and develop an inviting classroom where resiliency and cooperation are built, where learning is foremost and activity planning overcomes discipline and "social work." Provide a refuge for the abused and neglected child where competition and individual accomplishments are downplayed, but group triumphs are celebrated. Build a community where the abused child is not alone to tend to his wounds and doubt the significance of his existence, but is shown compassion and potential. This can be done without money, but educators are going to have to model risk taking for their students. And when that classroom is successful, build another, and another, until the school becomes a pioneering model. And when the entire school experiences success, *they* will come. The same politicians and wayward educational leaders who thought the best way to reform was by threat and embarrassment, will come to accept credit for the school's progress. Their quotes will be the first to be read in the newspapers because they did not get where they are by aligning themselves with failure. In the backs of their minds they will wonder what was done with the slow, under-achieving kids to get incredible test scores. "Are they teaching the test and test-taking techniques all semester long? Did the numbers improve because the testing pressure created an increase in dropouts? Did we find a way to eliminate compulsory attendance for traditionally weak sub groups?" It is then that the *real* educational leaders might describe the new school climate and classroom model. It is only then that they might show the self-proclaimed experts that a phrase like "No Child Left Behind" is not about measurement and accountability, it is actually a process built on compassion, cooperation, and stability. We will not worry about leaving children behind because they will voluntarily follow.

The problem, therefore, lies in the area of professional comfort and security. Is the leader willing to go against the grain and create a school many might initially view as an act of rebellion? Are the teachers supported enough to release the grip of discipline on classes and let them put the acquisition of facts on the back burner in lieu of intrinsic discovery? Of course, discipline of various degrees is a necessary evil, but has never been a method of motivation. Does the principal know enough about the effective classroom and have the power to convince his teachers that the extra effort will payoff in the long run? As with any sweeping change, and in most schools it would be just that, there will be doubt before there is return on the investment. Skeptics and veteran teachers who are set in their ways will be the last to board and the first to jump off. They will secretly undermine the process. They will need a leader who provides teachers with the encouragement and tools they will need. Staff development, resources, opportunities for collaboration and trade-off will be necessary.

Trade-off is the principal's obligation to the teacher much in the same manner the teacher compromises with the student. If a principal wants teachers to buy into his or her philosophy, then they must get something back. It is only fair. What can be done for each teacher to help resolve some of his or her frustrations? Are all duties necessary? Can some of the matter covered in faculty meetings be handled through e-mail, thus decreasing the need to meet as often and as long? Can two teachers per lunch period, for example, be allowed to eat in the teacher's lounge one week, and then two more the following week? That is a reward that also serves a purpose, because the teachers will share thoughts and ideas. Is there room in the budget to take the faculty bowling or cater a lunch on a workday? Can the school recruit parent volunteers to help teachers with tutoring, copying, and organizing events and activities? Could these parents monitor a class for fifteen minutes while that teacher observes a colleague?

In return, the teachers provide the school with cooperative learning, higher-order thinking skills, climate improvement, and increased collegiality. Lesson plans should then reflect large blocks of time dedicated to differentiation and essential questions on the higher orders of comprehension. Abused and neglected children can step from behind their defenses because fellow students and teachers take them by the hand, and probably have no idea how much they are helping. In fact, the process helps all, the givers and the receivers, dynamics that change depending on the circumstances.

The school becomes nothing more than a pyramid of support that is consistent with the vision and mission. This requires a large degree of creativity on the part of the professionals, finding ways to keep the school climate invigorating and new; however, individualization, free from fear of not fitting into a specific mold, is ownership. The time needed for extra planning can be found in the time saved by reduced disciplinary issues. This is the stuff that is sapped out of schools by top-down school administration, something that encourages perfunctory approaches to a mundane education. The way to accomplish this approach is through drills, repetition, order, competition, and measurement. Education is a process that empowers through a process of information application (not retention) and experience. Schools are not doing this consistently. Therein lies the problem.

OUT THE WINDOW

With all of the things the American society expects from teachers, it is important to note that these suggestions, such as building resiliency, do not involve additional responsibilities, just a willingness to utilize different capabilities. It is impossible to teach abused children resiliency in an adult environment that thrives on competition, labeling, test scores, and discipline. Teachers who are afraid to relinquish control of their classrooms reluctantly ignore their training and fearfully adopt the whimsical quick fixes of the educational reformists. They are in survival mode, like their abused children, front line soldiers being commanded by administrators and politicians who have either forgotten or never knew how learning occurs and resiliency is developed. Although this position may seem indirectly harsh on teachers, it is not the intent to expose anything other than their lack of proper training and guidance in lieu of imposed standards. In *The Right to Learn*, LindaDarling-Hammond states:

> They (teachers) are the aggregations of decisions made by textbook makers, test publishers, individual state agencies, legislatures, and school boards, often uninformed by professional knowledge, shared ideals, or consensual goals for education. Teachers are rarely involved in the professional activities of standards setting, curriculum development, or assessment.[14]

I am critical of the teachers' inability to properly perform their jobs because they are bombarded with fly-by-night overhauls, professional mandates, angry parents, duties and posts, stringent coaching and club sponsorship requirements, useless workshops, necessary second jobs, over-crowded classrooms, low public perception, and high turnover. Many of our teachers are uncertified or teaching on provisional contracts, bypassing clinical teacher training. Our soldiers on the front lines are weary, outnumbered, and unarmed. Yet the commanders, seeking public approval, threaten them with goals that would be easily surpassed if they gave them the training and support they need. Instead, they address the problem by raising the bar and formulating systems of accountability. Properly correcting the problem will take money and expertise, things our leaders seem to lack.

Building resiliency is nothing more than what happens to a child if he or she is exposed to good, effective teaching, which is a major theme in the school's ability to nurture abused and neglected children. Just because abused children may be more starved for the healing best teaching practices provide, that is not to assume that all children do not need to be fed. Basically, in a competitive, rewards-based school, only a few benefit and they do so at the expense of others. Abused and neglected children can become lost in the shuffle. However, if there is one thing a competitive society should understand, it is the concept of fairness. The competition that children face is currently inevitable, but not needed during early childhood through early adolescent development. Proper approaches that involve problem solving, cooperation, and hands-on activities ironically do a better job of preparing all children for the competitive world because resiliency and networking are being established, not humility and losing. The brain is flourishing, giving the learner confidence. So teachers do not teach resiliency, it simply happens when children learn in a supportive, child-centered environment where their contributions are just as important as those belonging to everyone else. Abused children develop self-worth, confidence, a trust in adults, and so many other essentials they can overcome nearly every aspect of their nightmarish home lives. Neglected children get attention, love, and other things that cannot be tested but will stay with them throughout their lives. They will learn to take chances without the fear of failing. If for no other reason than to save abused and neglected children, this should be happening in every single school in America; but the fact that it has been proven to benefit *all* children, makes it a must. If we must have our children compete, at least give them all the foundations to make it appear fair.

When I was enrolled in a nearby university about fifteen years ago, seeking teacher certification and a master's degree in English Education, I was somehow qualified to serve as a teacher on a provisional license. I had already been assigned the student-teaching duties that I was to begin in the spring. In the preceding November, however, that changed. I received a call from a principal who wanted me to interview for a teaching position at a nearby urban high school. Because I was young, married, and did not know how we were going to afford the loss of income student teaching would necessitate, I accepted the interview and later, the job. My advising professor in the teacher education program accompanied the morning of my first day to see the school and set up an observation schedule. He would observe me four times during the following semester.

Because enrollment at that high school was higher than anticipated, the principal had been granted an extra English teaching position about three weeks into the school year. He created the rosters for each of the classes by allowing teachers to select four or five students from each of their classes, literally creating an all-star team of thugs and drug dealers. I was assigned five classes, all lower level and at least one class from each grade. I was the third teacher hired to instruct this particular group of students in a three-month period; the first two quit and substitutes refused to take the assignment when asked. My debut, my defining moment had arrived before I was prepared to accept it, and I was about to meet 120 children who could drive the best, most experienced teachers to other careers.

Dr. Key and I walked up stairwells and down halls, looking for my room. I had been in the office all morning, and the students began arriving before I had the opportunity to get into my room. We found my door seconds before the bell rang, and my professor stopped me to give me one last bit of advice before I began the career I had spent three years preparing for by working days and attending night classes. I suppose I wanted the jolt of confidence a corner man would give a boxer moments before he steps into the ring, but he did just the opposite. He said, "Everything you learned, everything we taught you, throw it out the window. You have to be a drill sergeant here or they will eat you alive."

There were two doors to my classroom and most of the eleventh grade students wandered in late through the back while I nervously attempted to get my papers together. They stayed in the back of the classroom, assembled in a large circle, sitting on desktops and on the window ledge. They were all black males dressed in sagging pants and oversized baseball jerseys, with Malcolm X hats that were twisted sideways on their cornrows. In my most authoritative voice, I commanded, "Okay, class, if you will all come up here and take a seat, we can get started." They looked at me as if I had disrupted their normal routine. Then I heard a loud, sustained burst of laughter come from them. Even though I was only fifteen feet or so from them, my recollection makes them seem as if they were on the other end of a gym floor. I stood and walked toward them, not knowing what to do next, quickly assuming the posture of the drill sergeant Dr. Key recommended. One of the boys immediately stood out, deciding to use a barrage of profanity and sarcasm as his strategy for serving his peers as spokesperson and establishing himself as the leader of English III, section iv.

I remembered a few things from high school and the poultry-processing plant about situations like this. That helped me, but like the previous occurrences, it could have been painfully counterproductive. I knew that any sign of weakness would be like slapping a wolf in the face with a steak, so I confronted Tyree, their leader. "Step outside if you think you are man enough." The class erupted. This was quality entertainment for a Monday morning. I knew I had to get him away from his pack. I was never a math scholar, but even *my* calculations suggested that a one-on-one confrontation was better than twenty-two-on-one. "The rest of you better stay put. The principal has given me the right to call the resource officer and have you arrested if you decide to get cute." That was a lie, but they stayed, probably because they did not want to disrupt the drama that was quickly unfolding, or they feared violating their probations. The young man I had just singled out tried to laugh at the class as he looked back from the hallway, gesturing toward them that there was going to be a fight by punching his open left hand. I was already in the hall by that time, waiting impatiently for him to close the door. He did not, so I helped him out by slapping the door out of his hand, sending it hard into the jam inches from his face, rattling the glass lodged in the antique wood and sending a sonic boom down the hallway.

"What the fu-, are you crazy, mo fo?" He stood face to face with me, but his countenance had become angry, instead of amused as it had been before.

"You think this is your class? You think you can cuss me? You wanna try to act tough and bring that street crap into my classroom? You trying to get a rep at my expense?" I asked the questions as if at any minute I would crush his skull like an empty soda can. My lips were firm and I demanded eye contact. I inched closer to him, nearly trapping him between my chest and the wall. Colleagues I had yet to meet peeped into the hallway momentarily and closed their doors; they did not want anyone to know they had witnessed whatever it was I was doing. His face was now concerned more than angry, the kind of look a child gets when he is told that he has to eat his broccoli.

"You crazy, man."

"Yes I am. I also have the blessing of the principal to get you and all of your buddies taken out of here in cuffs if I have to. I can get you suspended for threatening me, which would probably land your ass in court."

"I ain't threaten you, man. You threatenin' me." He tried to walk away, but I grabbed his arm and pulled him back between me and the wall with an intended burst of strength. "Man, you better get yo' hands off me, man!"

I refused, squeezing his arm harder. I was only about 22 minutes into my career, so a resignation wouldn't exactly dip into my retirement account. "Let me tell you how it is. I could bring you out here and wallpaper the halls with you and nobody in this entire school would care. I drop you now and I am a hero because you are nothing to these people but a joke and a sorry piece of crap. Even your friends want to see me take you down because they want to laugh at you or at me; it doesn't matter. You better learn real quickly who it is you answer to, and then start doing it—NOW! Do you understand me?" No response. "DO YOU UNDERSTAND ME?" He reluctantly gave me the answer I wanted to hear, and I returned with him to the classroom. I didn't get much done that period, but eventually, everyone knew I had shaken Tyree up a little bit. In a weird way, it was as if he appreciated my concern or the manner in which I established respect the way it is earned in his world. I expected more trouble from him in the days and weeks that followed and it came as predicted, usually in spurts. However, the frequency of the conflicts diminished and his followers soon followed me. It was my personal experiences in a similar high school as a student and life experiences that prepared me for my first few weeks of teaching, not the teacher prep training at the university. However, Tyree had problems of his own and I saw it as my job to build him up after breaking him down.

Dr. Key knew that I had agreed to a nearly impossible task, and he knew that he was not equipped with the tools to help me. He observed growth in classroom behavior each time he visited, but after the third observation, he explained, "You have their attention, now teach them." I was afraid to loosen my grip. They were in rows and separated. They took a quiz after each lecture and were given worksheets every day. Most had been suspended as a result of my referrals by that time; I was winning. But I tried some of the approaches that I remembered enjoying when I was in school. The things that we discussed in college could now be applied: acting out plays, turning poems into songs, and letting them work in groups, the ultimate risk. I infused humor, pats on the back, and interest in their personal lives. I called their homes with good news and sent home positive letters. When Dr. Key returned for his fourth and final observation, we were concluding a unit on Romanticism, and the students were leading the review by discussing how their favorite quotes from Emerson and Thoreau could be applied to their lives.

It was my first year of teaching, one that should have sent me into another profession, but it was perhaps my most significant accomplishment to date. Even though I did things that were illegal, unethical, awkward, and unprofessional, I learned the hard way to speak in the language of the learner and to take chances with students. I had to trust my resiliency, which was beginning to teach me that there are few situations life can offer that I can not handle.

I suppose we all look for happy endings, which is rarely the case in the competitive arenas of education. Tyree wound up graduating, and pulled me into his group family hug after the ceremony, posing for a photograph that might still rest on his mother's mantle. Another student became a somewhat famous athlete, rising from a life on the streets where selling drugs was the primary activity. I do not take credit for either of these accomplishments, because it takes a village and, in the case of the latter, talent and luck.

One of the students in the class dropped out during the year; on the same day I signed his textbook back in, he killed a homeless man with a brick. Two others in that first period class were also convicted of murder for suffocating their aunt with a plastic bag because she wouldn't let them use the car. Another died the following year in a gang shootout. Three of them were among my better students.

I was hired because I was a male, a former college football player who would not be intimidated by this group. My job was to clean up the mess that the principal created by dumping students into these classes. I suppose it was not especially academically invigorating for them to be shoveled out of a lower-level English class and placed into a newly-created-just-for-them cellar that epitomized inferiority and rejection. I was fodder too. The principal did not seem to care if I developed into a teacher. I did that on my own, like so many teachers today. Unarmed, pushed to the front lines of the battlefield. What occurred is a testament to the powers of resiliency that I had inadvertently developed. For some of the students, I was able to help build some resiliency by utilizing differentiation, something that I did not think would work with this group. I still feel that I let most of the students down, however, only because I had limited knowledge, large numbers, and little support. On the other hand, I developed relationships that made a difference, and I did it all within the framework of good teaching. By allowing the children to see relevance in our activities, by allowing them to see their strengths in a class where interpreting literature was the tool and not the goal, I made Tyree's family photo at his high school graduation.

NOTES

1. C.L. Jew, K.E. Green, & June Kroger, "Development and Validation of a Measure of Resiliency," *Measurement and Evaluation in Counseling & Development*, 32, no. 2 (1999): 79.

2. Rexford Brown, *Schools of Thought.* (San Francisco: Jossey-Bass, 1993).

3. Robert Sullivan, "What Makes a Child Resilient?" *Time*, 157, no.11 (2001), 35–38.

4. Glenn Richardson,"High School Curriculum Fosters Resiliency," *Education Digest,* 63, no. 6 (1998): 23.

5. David Mrazek and Patricia. Mrazrek, "Resilience in Child Maltreatment Victims: A Conceptual Exploration," *Child Abuse and Neglect*, 11 (1987): 357–365.

6. Jew, Green, and Kroger, "Development", 75.

7. Jere Brophy, "Supporting Students' Confidence as Learners" *Motivating Students to Learn.* (Boston: McGraw-Hill, 1998): 57.

8. Marty Krovetz, "Fostering Resiliency," *Thrust for Educational Leadership*, 28, no. 5, (1999): 28.

9. Sue Howard and Bruce Johnson, "What makes the difference? Children and Teachers Talk about Resilient Outcomes for Children 'At-risk'," *Educational Studies*, 26, no. 3 (2000): 135.

10. Brown, *Schools of Thought,* 205.

11. Jim Hunt, *First in America: An Educational Governor Challenges North Carolina.* (Raleigh, NC: First in America Foundation, 2001): 15.

12. Hunt, *First in America,* 54.

13. Hunt, *First in America*, 55.

14. Linda Darling-Hammond, *The Right to Learn: A Blueprint for Creating Schools that Work* (San Francisco: Jossey-Bass, 1997): 213.

Chapter Seven

Arming the Educators

> "We think of our efficient teachers with a sense of recognition, but those who touched our humanity we remember with gratitude. Learning is the essential mineral, but warmth is the life-element for the child's soul, no less than for the growing plant."
>
> —Carl Gustov Jung, *The Gifted Child, Collected Works, Volume 17.*

AN EYE FOR ABUSE

The signal we send the public is characteristic of a dysfunctional society. We funnel millions of dollars each year into competitive, elitist school programs, but we seemingly disregard the abused and neglected. Is there evidence that the public money spent on elitist activities such as athletics and honor societies, programs that cut or exclude children, is exponentially higher than the funds, if any, designated to educate our teachers and school nurses to help put a stop to child abuse and neglect? Can we justify lotteries for the sake of children without properly funding interventions that could save many of them? Can we explain how a sophisticated culture where schools endorse spanking children who, quite possibly, are disobedient because they were whipped before arriving to school? Can we continue to pawn the problem off on federal and state agencies, like those in Scotland County, North Carolina, that investigated a whopping seven percent of reported abuse and neglect cases? Is there any way of knowing how widespread the problem actually is when most cases are rejected or misidentified? How many prisoners, alcoholics, drug addicts, homeless, and child abusers could have been saved by awareness and early interventions while in grade school? How many billions of dollars has child abuse cost this country?

Signs of abuse are overlooked every day in schools because teachers and administrators are not properly trained. Even in the event of the most obvious type of abuse, physical, the symptoms are frequently missed. It should also be noted that observing any of these obviously does not constitute neglect, but the teacher or school personnel should watch for patterns. Interrogating a child because he skinned his knee or said his daddy spanked him might offend parents and cause much more trouble than it is worth. Over-reactive adults in the school can cloud the waters and create so many exaggerated symptoms that the process loses credibility. However, erroneous assumptions or overzealous personnel will diminish with the proper training. Many experts and child supportive agencies recognize, with a strong consistency, obvious and subtle signs of child abuse. School employees have this training available, but seem to have opted for other forms of staff development. Recognition should be included in any faculty-wide training program, with the understanding that these characteristics are not exclusive to abused and neglected children, but a combination of these in conjunction with personal observations made over a brief period of time might qualify the case for participation in the school's established, investigative process. In other words, personnel must know what to look for, what to ask, and when to turn the case over to the proper authorities.

Prevent Child Abuse America recently published a comprehensive list entitled "Recognizing Child Abuse: What Parents Should Know." It might be the most concise yet thorough instrument of this nature developed to date. Teacher familiarity with it would increase awareness and serve as a basis for staff development. The following signs may signal the presence of child abuse or neglect. The first examples are subtleties to look for in the child, parent, and in an observation of their interaction:

> The child shows sudden changes in behavior or school performance. (He or she) has not received help for physical or medical problems brought to the parents' attention, has learning problems (or difficulty concentrating) that cannot be attributed to specific physical or psychological causes. (He or she) Is always watchful, has though preparing for something bad to happen, lacks adult supervision, is overly compliant, passive, or withdrawn. (He or she) comes to school or other activities early, stays late, and does not want to go home.[1]

An abusive parent might be one who basically ignores the child, blames her or him for all familial frustrations, or expects the child to accomplish more than they realistically can. This parent may assume all adults think as they do (as was the case with Phillip's father), and give the educator permission to use physical force or violence if the child continues to misbehave. It is extremely important to note that not all parents that fit this description are abusive, and all abusers do not necessarily fit this description.

Parents and students who rarely touch or look at one another, consider their relationship negative, or state that they do not like each other, might also suggest that there could be an underlying pattern of abuse in the home.[2] In relation to physical abuse (aside from the obvious bruises), the child may become frantic when parents are contacted and displays a lack of eagerness to go home. Fear is dominant and there is no sense of support from either party.

Signs of neglect are also visible, but teachers often overlook them. Again, these should be details used to decide whether one should investigate further, not to determine guilt or innocence, which is never the job of the educator. A child with dirty clothes and poor hygiene should cause a teacher to become curious. One should look for children without winter coats, those who are not receiving proper medical attention, or are sent to school when they are sick. Children who beg for or steal money, lack adequate school supplies, or are pulled from school for ridiculous reasons probably need to be watched more carefully. Of course, parents who are suspected or known to have a drug or alcohol dependency are much more likely to become abusive or neglectful than those who do not.[3]

Sexual abuse is difficult for educators because it is perhaps less tolerated than the other forms of abuse and rather difficult to detect, which makes the margin for error greater and elevates the cost of a mistake. *Prevent Child Abuse America* lists things to watch for that might make suspicions a little more concrete before interviewing a student or calling CPS:

- Experiences a sudden change in appetite.
- Demonstrates bizarre, sophisticated, or unusual sexual knowledge or behavior.
- Becomes pregnant or contracts a venereal disease, particularly if under age 14.
- Runs away.
- Has difficulty walking or sitting.
- Suddenly refuses to change for gym or to participate in physical activities.
- Reports nightmares or bedwetting.[4]

All forms of abuse are emotional. Emotional abuse, however, can be nonphysical, which makes if very difficult to distinguish. Perhaps the most common symptom is a lack of confidence and a warped ability to develop resiliency. These children tend to be detached from their parents and exhibit behaviors that fulfill their parents' negative image of them. If the educator is involved with the abused child's family, the adults will usually reveal abusive patterns because many do not consider their actions abusive, or they operate on misguided assumptions that their behavior can be easily justified to other adults.

With Alex and Phillip, I noticed bruises and cuts that were in various stages of healing. Had they not reported this to me, it was enough, in my mind, to constitute a pattern of injuries that gave me concrete legitimacy, more than a hunch or opinion, to file reports. With Alex, the cognitive underdevelopment was another factor that could mean that the abuse had been going on since infancy, but I would have never made that assumption without supporting symptoms. Both boys were substantially immature for their ages and were in special education classes, additional factors that might weight the equation.

I would never have concluded that Starla and David's problem was sexual assault or abuse had they not opened up to me. I initially misinterpreted their hostility toward one another, and if they had not told me, they would have been suspended for a minimum of five days. Ironically, since both parents worked and Steve was unemployed, they probably would have stayed with him during the suspension period.

THE SCIENCE OF ART

In April of 2005, my wife contacted me at school to let me know that I had just received a phone call from Robert Coles, responding to a letter I sent him a week earlier. I was inquiring about a technique he used in his book, *Their Eyes Meeting the World: The Drawings and Paintings of Children.* I rushed home to call him; for the past thirty years this professor of psychiatry and medical humanities at Harvard University has published over fifty books and sat with hundreds of children who were simply coloring and painting pictures he asked them to create. I was drawn to this Pulitzer Prize winner and his series of books called *Children of Crisis*, after reading Maxine Greene's *The Dialectic of Freedom*, in which she states, "Robert Coles . . . offered more clues as to how and why living beings reach for their freedom, even in the most fearful circumstances."[5] He described to me the manner in which children describe their world through art, and how he has been studying this phenomenon since Kennedy became president. After he briefly explained the technique, which is a process of listening to children through visual interpretation, I asked him if this is something only a psychologist or even a psychiatrist is qualified to do. "Absolutely not. Anybody who reads the book and can notice details that are very common in all children and, eventually, notice patterns." Art breaks the communicative barriers and allows the child to control every aspect of his or her self-expression. Neither he nor I suggest that a crayon drawing be the basis for calling CPS, but it creates a tool for understanding and a medium for the child to communicate beyond the constraints of words.

As educators, we sometimes forget to look at learning and dilemmas from the child's perspective, and sometimes the solutions to problems are found in play, when children's minds are the most active. By sitting with a child and having them draw and color pictures of family members, themselves, landscapes, and other common visuals, the child reveals things beyond the scope of words that may restrict communication and self-expression. *Their Eyes Meeting the World* describes how a boy explained this to Coles; he profoundly and eloquently stated, "When I draw, I try with all my might to concentrate, and that's when I do, because nothing is taking my attention away, and I don't have to speak."[6] With a minimum amount of training, school staff can learn to recognize the significance of lines, emotions in faces, color selections, proximity, the significance of the sun, and so many other details that would normally go unnoticed. When the teacher finds a particularly disturbing drawing, or one that needs elaboration, she casually and privately discusses the work with the child, giving him the concrete platform he needs to effectively overcome barriers that create sterile communications. For example, the teacher might ask, "Why are you and your sister crying?" The student then answers. "Because we cry together a lot." The teacher then has the opportunity to explore the reasons they cry together. That teacher might also ask, "Why is the tree purple and the sky orange?" "Why are their clouds over your house but not over anything else?" The answers may lead to a series of responses that reveal much more about a child than the conventional methods suggest.

There are other things that reveal internal impressions of the world around them that the child may not understand. To know the things that fascinate children in drawings and other forms of expression, like journal writing, is not only helpful to educators, but it should be a major indicator of how they learn and how teachers can reach all children. A child might draw himself with the ceiling right above his head and the walls at each shoulder. He uses black or navy crayons. It is dark and may indicate that he feels trapped. The fact that he had an entire page to explore but he chose to remain in a corner or other confined area of the page might reveal that he doesn't feel comfortable exploring or venturing out; he knows his place. Does this mean he is abused or neglected? Absolutely not, but it should mean the teacher needs to take a closer look and determine why the child made the choices he made.

Art analysis is futile without one-on-one contact with the student. Notice that the activity is hands-on and involves student-teacher communication. Cooperative exercises in language arts, social studies, music, science and even math classes can have the same impact, building on higher-order thinking and offering new insights to the self that might make problems solvable and increase confidence. Analyzing art is only one way a teacher can explore the darkest and most remote truths of an abused child's existence, but it must be done in a way that gives the control to the student. True teaching is more about reassuring and encouragement than it is the dissemination of trivia;

most of the data and facts educators dole out is inconsequential to anyone's life. It is more about listening than talking. It is more about observing than being viewed. Until then, teachers will miss the subtleties that contain the answers necessary to reach the abused and neglected children, sitting anonymously in rows, facing the front of the classroom, in chairs with tennis-ball slippers.

What does the modern school in America do with art? It creates competition. We give ribbons to kids like pumpkin farmers at the state fair. Educators sometimes frame a few works of art to go in the office because it evokes the same public relations warmth as the "Save the Children" tie Governor Jim Hunt wore on the cover of his book about test scores. We display fifteen pictures in the case from a class of twenty-two students. We have magnets made of children's drawings and send them home as fund raisers, each producing about $3.00 in profit. Little regard is given to the kids who do not receive ribbons, the seven students whose pictures were not displayed for lack of available space, or the rejection a child feels who has to return the magnet to school because the family didn't have the $5.00 to purchase it.

THE DELICATE NATURE OF INVESTIGATION

Teachers and administrators are encouraged to proceed with extreme caution if there is justifiable cause to seek more information concerning a suspected case of child abuse. Listening is the best method, but there may be a time when follow-up questions are needed, such as a response to an unusual comment or an injury that cannot be clearly explained. Safety is the first priority of the school and teacher, so ignoring signs or subtle pleas for help is intolerable. However, you cannot call in CPS every time little Billy skins his knee or Suzie stretches the truth. If questions need to be asked, they must be asked. However, it is important to remember that interviewing a child suspected of being abused is a very delicate matter. Questions must not lead, suggest, or reveal emotion or opinion. The abused child often wants to tell an adult; it is an issue of trust. Never surpass the amount of information needed to file a complaint with DSS or law enforcement. Also remember that the school employee may become emotionally overwhelmed, but those emotions should not hinder the process of collecting information objectively.

When dealing with a youth, one should be aware of that child's age and the abilities that coincide with normal cognitive and social development. The child's maturity level should also be taken into consideration, remembering the fact that emotional and physical abuse, sexual abuse, and neglect have caused substantial deficiencies in brain development. The interviewer is not to slant questions or non-verbally influence the child's answers due to the teacher's biased sympathy or assumptions. Shirley O'Brien, in an article entitled "A Heavy Price for Heroics" compiled a summary of the varied and age-significant cognitive abilities that an interviewer must take into consideration before addressing the child:

> Young children are egocentric. Swiss psychologist Jean Piaget states that children have difficulty seeing things from someone else's perspective until about the tenth grade, or their fifteenth birthday. Young children assume adults already know what is going on in their individual, unarticulated thoughts. Piaget also notes that young children are very quick to take the blame or feel guilt, especially when they are being questioned. The interviewer should remove that feeling and reassure the child that he or she is not to blame and should not feel guilty without leading the child to assign blame to the suspect.[7]

Pre-school and early elementary-level students are very literal thinkers who do not understand figurative or symbolic language. When questioning children of all ages we need to use a simple and direct language that may be substantially below their maturity level. Questions like, "If you were Huck Finn and your father had beaten you and locked you in a cabin, how would you react?" are poor questions. They are slanted, hypothetical, and involve a perspective other than that of the child. An understanding of the importance of concrete questions is vital, and equally important is the progression of question stem comprehension. "*What* and *where* questions develop first, usually between age three and four. *Who* questions develop next, followed by *when* and *why*. Finally, by age seven or eight, *whose* and *how* are comprehended."[8]

Children below the age of ten have enough difficulty recalling events, but if asked how they felt about a past event, the interviewer is more apt to get an uncertain answer. "Even as adults, feelings are often difficult to describe and interpret."[9] These questions might be appropriate for advanced investigators who understand the dynamics, but the school staff member must remember that their only objective is to establish a legitimate suspicion, not to build a case or determine guilt.

Short-term memory is not as developed as in adults, so the beginnings of elaborate sentences are often forgotten by the time the interviewer reaches the point or the question. They have difficulty with cause and effect relationships, so questions that begin with *if* and end with *then*, or those similar in structure, are not valid. "Children relate to single concepts."[10] It is important to keep sentences simple and the vocabulary below the level of the child to insure comprehension in a possibly stressful encounter with an interviewer. This is why an outline or checklist that is age appropriate would prevent confusion and bias coming out during the interview. CPS workers would be a good place to begin in developing the verbal questionnaires.

If the child senses what the interviewer wants to hear, then that child will try to answer in a manner that pleases the adult. They also believe that all adults tell the truth, so personal statements to the child or in the presence of the child are counterproductive. Interviewers who may be searching for a specific answer may repeat the question and finally arrive at the desired response. This will happen because children will lie or change answers to please adults. In school, for example, questions are repeated until a correct answer is given. They do not have the ability to separate the significance and differences between "two very dissimilar lines of questioning."[11]

If the school system develops a solid technique of interviewing, then CPS can spend more time investigating and less time screening. Forms from the interview can be signed and faxed to CPS, eliminating time consuming question and answer sessions between the reporting adult and the caseworker. CPS has a regiment of questions they routinely ask, so the questionnaire should also include answers to those questions, which can be completed before the interview with the child. Unless the school system and CPS have clauses making the practice permissible, video and audio tapes should not be recorded, even if the parent signs a consent form, which is highly unlikely. Many times the consent form is only applicable to certain situations that are not handled by the school.

To add to these points, in our society there is a fine line between child abuse and corporal punishment, even though my personal beliefs do not acknowledge one. To me, spanking teaches children that adults solve problems with violence, even though the child's misdeed might have been peaceful in nature. Again, the child's learning is not intrinsic with spankings; it teaches them to fear pain as well as the adult who administers the discipline. Sure it works, because the change is usually immediate, but the long-term, underlying effects on the child and the child-adult relationship are altered. Trust is compromised. Children are coerced into a forced behavior, where the only real consequence becomes getting caught. When the lesson is not intrinsic, when it is not based on communication and understanding, it becomes one of survival. Lying can become acceptable because the establishment of trust is compromised; it is the avoidance of physical pain that is central to the child's approach. Sure, some parents may preach and yell before and after beatings like my father did, but that simply intensified control and hostility. There was no dialogue. I learned to ignore the difference between right and wrong because there were instances when I was innocent and still beaten. Sure it happens in homes, but the fact that some schools still use corporal punishment is astounding.

I realize this now, but abuse beyond a normal spanking was my normalcy as a child. I didn't realize that my childhood was that different than those of my friends, so I didn't know to speak out and my teachers did not develop networks of communication and cooperation. I learned those things through athletics (beyond the cut-throat competition, there are redeemable aspects of being a part of a team that parallels the ideal classroom model) and Mr. Michael's class. I was withdrawn, guilt-ridden, and unconfident. Without the nurturing and support provided in his class and through teamwork, I had no outlet. Although some children in a nurturing school environment will try to describe abuse in segments and fragments, it remains the adult's responsibility to use his or her professional training and knowledge of childhood cognitive, social, and linguistic development to dismiss or reinforce accurately suspicions and take proper action. Informing children about child abuse and neglect is a part of the communication network. They need to know what is acceptable and what is not. A program added to the health curriculum, along with contacts in the school to assist the child who may have a report or questions, would contribute to safe schools and provide an outlet for the child to come forward. In essence, educate the children and give them the path to seek and find help.

Resource or police officers must remember laws about questioning children without an adult present, which is also why school employees need to follow procedures developed and approved by the local CPS officials. According to the "National Study of Child Protective Service Systems and Reform Efforts," published for the U.S. Department of Health and Human Services, CPS recommends required training "on CPS of local community professionals." Since school employees spend more time with children than any other adults except perhaps, the parents, it would be beneficial that all school employees get trained in several areas of child abuse detection, prevention and confidentiality. Guidance counselors need training in PTSD, and regular counseling should be set up once the report is verified and accepted by CPS. If CPS is not going to be properly funded, it needs to establish relationships and cooperation with the schools to help overcome that obstacle.

KNIGHT OF THE ROUND TABLES

David Purpel is a former professor whose Socratic classroom strategies made no sense to me at the time because the class was called "Curriculum Planning," a bit misleading because it was philosophy and little more. There was no "planning." I left after the first session wondering how I was ever going to apply the rhetoric, something I enjoyed very much, to developing curriculum.

However, the brilliance of his teaching unfolded as my mind became open to the broadness of the concept of curriculum. He began the class by having us define curriculum, something we found surprisingly difficult. As our frustrations increased, we became more interested in his definition than our own. He never told us, and I became somewhat agitated because I had already paid my tuition. Upon reflection, I realized that we sought a standard definition of curriculum when that answer could only be found to have meaning if we created the definition ourselves.

As a true educational leader, was I to follow the blueprints of our predecessors or blaze a trail based on new thinking? He seemed to suggest that there was a conflict in education reform between the brain and the heart, and our leaders have been too afraid to listen to the latter. But he never answered our questions unless the answer led to a more complex one. So we explored possibilities from various perspectives and formed rich meanings to abstract concepts and theories. He was a true teacher and a brilliant philosopher. His handling of the issue of competition in his body of published work is made more powerful because it requires an inspection of the heart, where truth is more readily found. This is the ingredient that cannot be legislated. This is what our leaders do not seem to understand because it is immeasurable and lost to the arenas of competition, where they earn their livelihoods.

If we cannot turn to the political or business leaders, then we must look another direction. Educational leaders are influenced by the aforementioned, and they are so extrinsically trained in antiquated methods that even they may not have the answer even if extricated from the political red tape. Meaningless words, such as "No Child Left Behind," have become no more than an example of the paradox between reality and educational policy. We need leaders who do not fallaciously attempt to measure the immeasurable by developing high-stakes testing to produce data for leaders to manipulate in an effort to hoodwink the public. It is easier to get re-elected that way, for true educational reform will take generations and is to be an ongoing process, and there is no way to garner exclusive personal credit over that period of time. It would have to be a collective humanitarian effort where the leadership is shared and even sacrificed for the good of the cause. The leaders we need to model are the humble humanitarians, not the brash politicians.

Purpel makes this point:

> As a profession we are obligated to be models and to affirm models for ourselves. The greatest models of teachers have been religious figures-people like Moses, Jesus, Buddha, Dietrich Bonhoeffer, Martin Luther King, and Mohandas Gandhi-who have inspired millions upon millions to be guided in their lives by a vision that provides light, warmth, and transcendence. It is to participate in this task, however humbly, however inadequately, that enables our work to be worthy of being considered sacred.[12]

At some point, we have gotten away from the meaning of education and created a competitive factory that mass-produces Pavlovian dogs in a quest for a sole objective, to elevate test scores that will later, in some minds, translate into professional productivity. The seed for standardized testing was planted before the ink on *A Nation at Risk* was dry, a document that does not try to hide the fact that our schools need to improve if we are to compete on a global scale. High stakes testing has evolved from a fear that we would lose our supremacy in the world order and our inferiority would threaten national security. It is time to take back our children from the governmental control and begin working on a child-centered approach to educational reform that focuses on the balance, esteem, and contributions of all children to a common good. For the moment, abused and neglected children are destined to lead unfruitful lives full of regret and crisis. We are systemically burying them from the time they learn to walk by forcing them to measure up to others. Which is why we are closer to the practices of Hitler and Stalin than we are to those of Gandhi or Jesus.

When my youngest son Garrett was six and his brother Taylor was in the third grade, the entire family went to the grand opening of their new school on the eve of the first day it would open its doors. We went down the first-grade hall as soon as we arrived, passing other families who were looking at posted rosters beside the teachers' classrooms. Garrett recognized his name on a brightly-colored, alphabetized list and flew into the room, where several of his future classmates were clustered together on the floor, pulling out educational toys and cooperatively trying to figure them out. Garrett bounced from center to center, like he had just won everything there and was trying to comprehend his newly acquired wealth. There were five circular tables with five tiny seats pushed underneath each, the legs of every chair adorned with four, optic-yellow, tennis-ball slippers. He jumped from one round table in the room to another, again looking for his name to see where he would sit. He went to the blue table first, and then the red, finally finding his name on the green table in the center of the room. He spied the names of his four partners written in vivacious letters on tags adorned with tropical birds, and he adopted these strangers who were certain to be a huge part of his life the following day. He looked at us and smiled the grin he gets when he embarrassingly tries not to show his enthusiasm but can't contain it; he would curl his upper and lower lips around his teeth and open his mouth. Rather strange. This was probably my fault for teasing him about Barney and then the Power Rangers; he was the youngest and probably thought we would tease him about his classroom, which looked an awfully lot like Pee Wee Herman's Playhouse or an under-funded Chucky Cheese pizza restaurant/theme park. I didn't harass him because I was excited too, having squandered most of my childhood in the dark alleys of fear and shame. I was also drawn to the inviting warmth and hospitality of the room. It was an exciting, vividly-colored, happy place, one that I was not familiar with, having spent eleven years as a high school English teacher and one as a middle school assistant principal. It was refreshing to see students ecstatic about the opening of school. I wondered, when I looked at the sprawling children playing in the floor, exactly when it is that educators abandon them, when these children lose the spirit of discovery and become morbid creatures of routine and solitude.

Garrett disappeared a few times during our brief conversation with the teacher, but he quickly reappeared in the math corner working out a problem with a member of the red round table and then on the rug with a book under the huge "Reading Rainbow." It took several attempts, but he eventually and reluctantly came when we summoned him to follow us to Taylor's third grade classroom.

Taylor's teacher, posted at the entrance to the classroom like a guard, was pleasant but formal, immediately telling us that this was a big year for our son and his fellow third graders because it would be the first year of state standardized testing. She explained that he would be pre-tested in August in order to determine his reading and math aptitudes, so they could form the ability-level groups and gauge the growth from the year's beginning to its end. Garrett wasn't paying attention; he was excitedly waiting for us to get out of the doorway that we clogged talking to the teacher. Eventually My wife Cindy, Taylor, and I seeped into the uninviting enclosure that was the antithesis of the room we previously visited. Taylor, whose facial expressions have always been honest windows, was stoic. Desks were aligned like soldiers in perfect formation, four rows of seven facing the front, which was equipped with an overhead projector and a white board with blue marker scribbling depicting the first day's date and objectives. There was also a bulletin board beside the door that rather impersonally greeted the children because they could not see it until they were already in the room. "Welcome Bearcats" it cleverly stated on a yellow background with blue script, framed into the cork by a stream of what bearcat paw prints must look like if bearcats actually existed.

The mood of the classroom was somber and the chatter of others slightly echoed against the tile and painted cinderblock walls, as if they were speaking into an empty barrel. Garrett finally burst into the room from the hallway, still excited about the glimpse of his immediate future on the first grade hall. Not three steps in, he froze, slowly looking around the classroom as if another sudden movement would trigger an alarm. He curiously glanced at us as if we were in the wrong place and should escape before something tragic happens. His face, also not yet adept at hiding his feelings, lost all traces of glee as it gave in to the reality of his brother's and his institutional prophecy. He sympathetically gazed at Taylor, who also was obviously not impressed with the differences between his classroom and Garrett's. "Taylor," he said in a troubled voice that revealed trace amounts of both shock and empathy, "how can you have school with no round tables?"

CLIMATE CONTROL

There is some debate as to whether resiliency is inherent or procedural. I suppose it parallels other meaningless philosophical debates because the source is not the issue. To suggest that resiliency is not inherent, but a learned skill is silly, considering the fact that so much of it is cognitive and subconscious. It is innate but must be nurtured. It is as much a part of human growth as anything else. To extend a previous metaphor, it is a seed and environmental factors help nourish or hinder its development. The seed itself has the components to grow, but depends on its surroundings to develop. If the environment at home is stunting a child's growth, then it is up to educators to provide the right balance of sunlight, water, and soil to make it grow. From this perspective, educators are environmentalists anyway, providing the proper conditions to stimulate learning. Therefore, as a horticulturist, the teacher must provide the balance for each plant. If no stalk or sprig is to be left behind, then a good farmer will know what abilities each possesses and what each needs. That is true from the recognition of the deficiency until the removal of the stakes for the weaker plants, when they are strong enough to support themselves, when their roots now provide stability and nourishment independently, when they become self-sufficient. This must be the farmer's ultimate goal or his crop is diminished; when he knows that he has done all he can, he then places the once frail seedling into the uncontrolled elements with the ability to prosper.

In doing so, the farmer gives the plant the will and the strength to overcome obstacles, the power to embrace adversity, and the stability to grow. He does not spend his time teaching it how to extract water through its roots or how to reach toward the sun. These things will be figured out when the strength and courage are in place. Nor does he expect the young and weak seedlings to be able to withstand the summer heat, even though they will soon stand tall in July. But we expect our developing children to compete because the adult world is about competition. There is no need for foundation building or development; they must compete in order to be successful, which seems to be the unquestioned assumption. When we attempt to build foundations in competitive soil, we fail, just as the farmer who plants his crop too late, exposing the seedlings to the brutality of the competitive heat before they are ready. Of course, farmers know better and plant when the temperature is mild and will gradually increase along with the abilities of the plant. If farmers understand this, and I am sure failure somewhere along the line taught them this, why do educators continue to lose such a large percentage of their crop every year without adjusting the climate, something the farmer cannot control? Instead, politicians and educational leaders add excessive water and fertilizer because what benefits one must benefit all.

In the classroom, learning the content has become the objective when it should not be. Paulo Freire calls the teacher-centered classes that are prevalent in most modern classrooms (in fact, the higher the grade the more prevalent it becomes), "banking education." He says, "Education is suffering from narration sickness. . . . Words are emptied of their concreteness and become a hollow, alienated, and alienating verbosity."[13] Overcoming the obstacles that lead to understanding how to apply the lesson learned to other situations is, quite simply, learning. Content is just the obstacle course, the game pieces, and not the strategy. Purpel states:

> Education must treat each student as a meaning-seeking and meaning-creating individual, enabling the learner to develop a critical, passionate, and nourishing engagement with oneself, one's culture, and with the natural world. The curriculum should be organized around life's fundamental questions and the serious moral and existential concerns of young people.[14]

Purpel is referring to things that contribute to resiliency and the things that all children, especially the abused and neglected, need to succeed. However, he is describing not a fad or a twelve-step program, he is telling us that education must nurture and be pertinent to the child for true learning to take place. These things are not easily converted to data that can then be manipulated into bar graphs and pie charts that can then be used to persuade the voting public. It is art.

Therefore, after schools acknowledge that child abuse exists and it serves the child's best interest to assist in the development of resiliency, teachers need the tools and the knowledge to teach. They need development in hands-on activities and resources to give them *new* ideas, they need collaborative opportunities to brainstorm and share *great* ideas. Teachers need support and encouragement to take chances. Perhaps it is best phrased this way: educators need leadership that will help them establish professional resiliency, so they will have the courage and vision needed to help children become self-sufficient learners and build personal resiliency. Teachers need to be practitioners, talented in developing strengths in children and eliminating fear of failure. To do this, the well-intending political abuse, the mandated standardized testing, will have to be ignored, or stopped.

According to Marty Krovetz, "Schools must foster resiliency for the adults in the school community if they are to foster resiliency for students."[15] Giving the teachers the same growth opportunities offered to students can do this. In his article entitled "Resiliency: A Key Element for Supporting Youth At-Risk," Krovetz describes ways in which principals can achieve this goal:

1. *Increase collegiality*. By increasing collegiality, teachers learn to function as a cooperative team, seeing one another as resources. Time needs to be reserved for teachers to have unstructured time with little formatting, just a topic.
2. *Give teachers a voice*. Democratic government of schools increases morale, ownership, and faculty belonging.
3. *Increase job satisfaction*. Positive approaches to teaching and learning turn gripe sessions into productive interactions.[16]

For now, teachers need to remain true to their craft and merely humor the "top-down" reform efforts. Forget about test scores and competitive stressors. Instead, build an environment that includes, "social skills training, self-monitoring, self-evaluation, and self-reinforcing strategies."[17] Perry simplifies the entire process:"Resilience cannot exist without hope."[18]

A fictional scenario might illustrate this more clearly:

> Over the past three weeks, Steven's grade dropped from 88 to 71. Mrs. Jones reviewed her grade book and notices that he doesn't do his homework and the poster board project was never turned in. Steven's mother did not come in for a conference after school, so Ms. Jones had no choice but to give Steven a D. She was fair, providing the opportunity to hand in the missing work late, with a small penalty. Steven never turned it in, and Mrs. Jones didn't mind dropping the grade because although Steven is very smart, his attitude is bad, he disrespects adults, and he doesn't care about school.

Mrs. Jones didn't realize it, but she was doing nothing more than kicking a fallen child. On paper, she had recorded interventions and multiple opportunities to redo work; after all, the project grade would have been an easy A+ if only handed in on time. She did not notice that the source of Steven's grade reduction was homework. She probably had no idea that Steven was being neglected because his father was arrested for beating his mother. She never knew that Steven's mother did not attend the conference because she has been looking for jobs to support the family and worked evenings. Chances are she had no clue that Steven could not afford the cardboard and markers for the project, or that the power had been cut off in his apartment for the past six days; homework is more difficult in the dark.

Projects and homework grades are common practices in schools and intended to reinforce the teachings that occur in the classroom. With Steven, they reinforced the things that were occurring in the home. Steven could not compete with the other poster board projects that were expensively created by supportive parents. His homework was often attempted amidst blood curdling arguments and physical violence. He had no access to a computer or even school supplies. His lights don't work and he is often cold. His mother is out job hunting and he has three younger brothers and sisters to watch. What could have Mrs. Jones done differently?

When focus is centered on anything but the child, then it is not focus at all-it is interference. Mrs. Jones cannot fix Steven's problems at home, but she can fix the environment at school. Perhaps her classroom is more competitive than it should be; perhaps her grading practices are more norm-referenced (comparative) than she realizes. Perhaps there is no system of support for the child to express concerns, fears, or communicate difficulties completing assignments. Perhaps he is not given the opportunity to feel the strength of an extended family and establish a trusting relationship with an adult. It isn't measurable, but cooperative classrooms have the power to overcome just about any tragic circumstance. They are that strong.

Garrett loved his first-grade classroom with the round tables. I loved my high school English class with the round-table discussions. With the exception of the one-piece desk manufacturers, who benefits when round tables are removed from our classrooms? The most significant component in building resiliency in abused and neglected students is cooperative learning. "It requires the child to develop good judgment, respect for others, harmony, and flexibility."[19] It is also the best way to turn competitors into resources. When dealing with a suspected abused child, the teacher might go as far as match him with another who compliments his personality and learning style; it would build his confidence and perhaps establish a friendship. When teachers insist on being the centers of attention, it denies the children the wonderment of exploration, the lessons of failed and converted effort, and ultimately, the exhilaration of discovery. It is erroneous for a teacher to choose synopsis over discussion. Student questions are always more important than teachers' answers. Unfortunately, this has been explained to teachers for years, but it seems many teachers are afraid to relinquish control. We resort back to our safe, comfort zones where product-centered learning is possible when heavy-handed disciplinary structure is in place.

In *The Paideia Program: An Educational Syllabus*, a movement that features cooperation and Socratic classrooms, it states:

> The main goal of *The Paideia Proposal* as an educational manifesto calling for radical reform of basic schooling in the United States is to overcome the elitism

> of our school system from its beginning to the present day, and to replace it with a truly democratic system that aims not only to improve the quality of basic schooling but also aims to make that quality accessible to all children.[20]

Within the cooperative groups, a solid lesson plan that focuses on problem-solving skills allows the children to share strengths to overcome individual weaknesses. It is difficult to design cooperative activities of this nature without a natural progression toward higher-level thinking weaving its way through the fabric of the teacher's creativity and knowledge of the students. Opportunities for participation give the student a feeing of belonging. Teacher-centered instruction, on the other hand, intensifies the crippling process of the abused and neglected child because it models adult dominance over children. It is supported by consequences and robs the child of the opportunity for introspection and a personalization of the material. Cooperative projects are not centered on the ability to answer questions correctly with the focus and attention on the mistakes, but it allows for positive acceptance, effort, and relationship building through the group's formation of the questions. Rubrics and conferences guide the process where evaluation is a face-to-face celebration of strengths and how those strengths can improve weak areas. The interaction with learning teams and the one-on-one teacher conferences builds the learning network and increases the child's feelings of self-worth and importance. "Nothing replaces the security that comes from a child having a close, personal relationship with a significant adult."[21] These things are important for all students, but they are crucial for abused and neglected children. They transform competitors into teammates. They allow for student exploration and social development. They are fun, and they happen around round tables.

MAKING SENSE

Although the problems that are crippling abused and neglected children are deeply embedded into our schools, the solution requires no additional funding, special labels or extra programs. Good teaching has always been good teaching, but the art is being blind-sided by legislative demands and incompetent school boards. Although educators have little control over these components, which suggests that these elements should be, for the most part, ignored. The leaders will get their petty test scores that show dramatic improvement because our children and teachers will be building resiliency, community, and cognitions that exceed the minimal requirements of standardized testing. Politicians will congratulate the teachers (out of one side of their mouths) who are hidden in the limelight's shadow that the politicians created when they stepped into it, reminding the public of the vague and empty proclamations they made during their last campaigns. Let these adults compete for shallow accolades; it is what they have been conditioned to do. Save the abused children and so many more students will be enhanced by the same net. Ignore the politicians, because many lack the training to know what facilitates the various forms of human development. They either take action ignorantly or place complete confidence on the comments of advisors. Therefore, they are either morons or parrots, but not farmers.

It must begin with leaders, superintendents who are clever enough to appease the morons and parrots and pioneer these proven practices. Everything comes back to a circular progression, like the round tables in Garrett's classroom that inspired a sense of enthusiasm and excitement. Warren Bennis has strong and meaningful words that are applicable to what superintendents need to do to extricate themselves from the strings of the political puppeteers:

> The point is to become yourself, and use yourself completely—all your skills, gifts, and energies—in order to make your vision manifest. You must withhold nothing. You must, in sum, become the person you started out to be, and enjoy the process of becoming.[22]

This *is* the vision, and this passage applies to every principal, teacher, and student in our public schools. The circle of learning, discovery, and rediscovery. The network of community. The power of cooperation. Nonconformity. Resiliency. Round tables.

NOTES

1. "What Parents Should Know," *Prevent Child Abuse America* <www.preventchildabuse.org/publications/parents/downloads/recognizing_abuse.pdf> (2003).
2. "What Parents Should Know."
3. "What Parents Should Know."
4. "What Parents Should Know."
5. Maxine Greene, *The Dialectic of Freedom* (New York: Teacher's College Press, 1988):102.
6. Robert Coles, *Their Eyes Meeting the World: The Drawings and Paintings of Children* (New York: Houghton Mifflin, 1992): 7.
7. Shirley O'Brien, "A Heavy Price for Heroics," *The Association for Childhood International* <http://www.udel.edu/bateman/acei/childabuse.pdf> (1991): 4.
8. O'Brien, "Heavy Price," 4.
9. O'Brien, "Heavy Price," 4.

10. O'Brien, "Heavy Price," 5.

11. O'Brien, "Heavy Price," 5.

12. David Purpel, *The Moral and Spiritual Crisis in Education: A Curriculum for Social Justice and Compassion,* (New York: Bergin and Garvey, 1989).

13. Paulo Friere, *Pedagogy of the Oppressed* (New York: Continuum, 2003): 71.

14. Purpel, *The Moral and Spiritual Crisis in Education: A Curriculum for Social Justice and Compassion.*

15. Marty Krovetz, "Resiliency: A Key Element for Supporting Youth At-risk," *The Clearing House* 73, no. 2 (1999): 121.

16. Krovetz, "Resiliency," 123.

17. Yolanda Padron, Hesholt Waxman, and Shwu-Yong Huang, "Classroom Behaviors and Learning Environment Differences Between Resilient and Nonresilient Elementary School Students," *Journal of Education for Students Placed at Risk* 4, no. 1, (1999): 65–82.

18. Bruce Perry, "How Children Become Resilient," *Scholastic Parent and Child,* 10, no. 2 (2002): 33.

19. R. H. Lock and M. Janas, "Build Resiliency," *Intervention in School & Clinic* 38, no. 2 (2002): 117.

20. Mortimer Adler, *The Paideia Program: An Educational Syllabus* (New York: MacMillan, 1984): 1.

21. Lock and Janas, "Build Resiliency," 117.

22. Warren Bennis, *On Becoming a Leader* (New York: Basic Books, 2003): 104.

Chapter Eight

Flight

"This above all: To thine own self be true."

—William Shakespeare, *Hamlet*

PHILLIP

The heat from the asphalt liquefied distant vehicles as my boys and I cruised down Highway 52 with the windows down, slurping Big Gulps during a sunny July afternoon. I veered into the left turn lane and stopped at a red light, as the gale-force wind in my new, 4-door Toyota Tacoma halted with the truck. The volume of my Meatloaf CD was suddenly blaring too loudly without the distortion of the road noise and breeze. As the mangled-hair duo yelled to one another in the back seat in an attempt to communicate over "Paradise by the Dashboard Lights," I nervously scanned the other vehicles coming to a standstill around us, probably because I wasn't comfortable exhibiting such a pitiful combination of poor parenting and mid-life crisis. The boys' heads bounced with each twang of the electric guitar because that is what we did when we decided to get Big Gulps, roll down the windows, and cruise steaming streets with nothing more to do than share this brand of rock, forged during my prime but twenty years before their births, with our hometown. School was out for summer and my month-long break had begun, so it was time to let our city know that the boys were back in town, but I didn't have the CD with the song by that name, so we appropriately selected a suitable alternate from Meatloaf's *Bat Out of Hell* collection.

A loud, rumbling, and smoky vehicle inelegantly pulled ahead of us into the lane that went straight. The stench from the muffler-less pickup, which was also manufactured about twenty years before Garrett and Taylor were born, rudely filled our cab and its din drowned out our pitiful singing. We rolled up the windows and turned on the air conditioning and the stereo down, as the wounded truck sputtered and slipped into a murmuring coma. The rusted and twisted bumper supported no tailgate, but at the back of the bed, with backs pressed against the rear of the cab, sat two boys with a big dog between them, facing us, except when they stretched over the edge to spit tobacco juice onto the sizzling road. They were laughing and stroking their pet as if it were an Egyptian deity and they its humble servants, as if its sagging, dripping tongue were the source of all wisdom and bountiful harvests.

If anyone had been staring at us when we pulled up to the intersection, they weren't any more. The scene resembled something from *Deliverance*, but with less civility and sophistication. One of the bed-ridden boys looked at us and raised a cautious hand to timidly wave. I realized then that it was Phillip, who apparently wasn't sure if I was Mr. Neal. His faint smile instantly grew when I acknowledged his greeting. The left turn lane light changed to green and I crept by his truck, momentarily stopping and rolling down my electric, passenger-side window with nothing in mind to say. His left jaw protruded with a man-sized chew that muffled his normal impediment and strong Southern drawl, but I think he said, "What's up, Mr. O'Neal!"

Through my rearview mirror my children seemed stunned that I would stop to talk to such a creature; it countered everything I had ever told them about locking doors and not speaking to people of similar pedigrees. They stared at Phillip, his brother, and the dog as if the paramedics would soon arrive to rescue the shabby group from the wreckage on which they sat, or perhaps a tow truck to save the wreckage from them. I peered back at my one-time-project who had moved away several months earlier. He was grinning at me.

I responded, "Hey, Phillip! Good to see you. How did you do in school this year?" The car behind me blew the horn because the arrow hovering above my truck glistened green while I sat in the turn lane.

"None too good, I don't reckon. But it don't matter. I ain't goin' to no summer school either. But I passed anyway!"

And he will again next year, and the next, until he quits. "Congratulations, Phillip!"

"What?"

I figured the noise of the truck buried my words. I yelled louder. "Congratulations, Phillip!" He had to hear that, I thought.

"What?"

The car behind blew the horn again. I started to wave and roll away, when it dawned on me, this was Phillip I was talking to. I rephrased, "Good job!"

"Thanks!" he replied as I exited his life again. I gazed into the cab of the old white and blue, two-tone Chevrolet with a chalky hood as I rode by, and glimpsed a hairy arm hanging out of the rolled-down window just behind the glassless side-view mirror frame. A sweaty, bare shoulder led my eye to the greasy head of Phillip's father, tilted back to finish the last sip from a can of Budweiser. The light turned yellow, so I sprinted through the intersection, much to the disturbance of the silver Honda behind us, the one with the annoying horn problem.

A foreboding mood consumed me instantly. Phillip's presence flashed me back to our ordeal and ruined the festivity of my excursion. In my rear-view mirror I saw their truck scamper across the intersection like a comet with a black, smoky tail. I turned the CD player back up, now on "Two out of Three Ain't Bad." Before my sons and I rode over the hill ahead of us, I remember wondering if the dog between Phillip and his brother, the one with the enchanting tongue, was Rocky. I somberly compared Phillip's dad to me, both in our pick-ups, both sipping on beverages with our boys in the back, both with seemingly no particular destination in mind, just different paths and different circumstances. My boys were sitting in the back seat and buckled in, his boys sliding around in the bed of a dented and shattered truck. My boys securely ascended into the civilization just ahead, while his disappeared behind an oily smokescreen on a nameless, downwardly-sloping country road, winding its way through the pungent aroma of turkey houses and furrowed fields that seemed to go on forever.

TREY

Trey's story is perhaps more climactic than Phillip's, which might be more satisfying for those who demand closure, even where there is none. Summer rolled by and he found himself walking the streets of my neighborhood with younger children, probably because there weren't any others his age. There were occasions when he would turn up at my house, but I usually had to run him away because he would curse or break something that belonged to my boys. He allowed his hair to grow longer and even more into his eyes than before, which seemed to accentuate his hunching posture. He never wore shorts even though the humidity was high and the thermometer was bouncing on 90 degrees in the breezeless shade, opting instead for frayed blue jeans that nearly covered his skateboarding shoes completely. An oversized tee shirt completed his ensemble, reminding my children of "Shaggy" from *Scooby Doo*. It was nearly impossible to see him pass by the window on his way down the street without being reminded of the awards day a few weeks before. I wondered if he ever thought of it, or if he had locked it away with similar memories. Nonetheless, summer passed slowly and he seemed to slip deeper into his prophetic persona, one that became darker as the days grew longer.

Before he was ready, fall arrived and the school bus began squeaking to a stop every morning at his house. With red lights flashing and horn blowing, he would crawl into its ear and slide into the back seat. Most mornings I would see him waiting there for his bus and it would make me very happy; it meant that I wouldn't get stuck behind the yellow, lumbering monstrosity on my way to work. On the miserable days when I *was* late, it seemed as if the bus stopped every twenty feet and picked up kindergarten students whose parents were suffering from acute separation anxiety, holding their adorable treasures and kissing them again and again before they too were swallowed by the diesel-fueled behemoth. It was touching every time I saw it, all sixteen times each morning, if I didn't get out of my driveway in time. When I heard the horn blast and the intimidating exhaling of the air brakes at Trey's house and saw the fire-red eyes that blinked at me fervently, I knew I had to frantically start the car and beat the bus before it slithered past my driveway. It was like playing chicken with a dragon, but most days I pulled it off. If I lost the race for positioning, not only was I delayed, I got to learn sign language by exchanging meaningless, nonverbal gestures with students clustered around the back windows of the bus, anxiously looking at me as if I wanted them to.

Trey attended a Kindergarten through eighth grade school that enrolls fewer than 400 students, so there were teenagers and five-year-olds riding the same buses. He was in the seventh grade at the beginning of this school year but he was still two years behind schedule, so he was the age of a high school freshman. It must have been humiliating. I felt sorry for him because I knew that he was living within the psychological framework of abuse, but until treated, he was a threat to others. I knew what he was capable of becoming; I knew the chaotic rage that manifested itself silently in his mind. Since I was not in a position to help him, I protected my children from him as much as I felt necessary. Upon reflection, I wish I had done more, but I am sure my intentions would have been insulting or embarrassing. So I watched a boy implode when I could have saved him. I will always wonder if I could have been his Mr. Michael. It was sobering to later learn that there would be no tomorrows, no second chances to save Trey from himself.

Months later I noticed that Trey was no longer getting on the bus at his house. In fact, according to a neighbor, Trey didn't attend school any more. It occurred to me that I was no longer seeing him plodding down the street as he blindly gazed into our windows. I was informed that Trey had some problems on the bus, and this year he would fall short of repeating his graciously shared title of "Outstanding Bus Rider" at the awards ceremony. He would be anxiously awaiting his name to be called that May, but the presenter behind the voice would be a juvenile judge.

Trey sometimes shared seats with the kindergarten students to make room for everyone when "three to a seat" was needed. Because buses are limited and the route crowded, it was practical to have small children sit with the bigger ones to accommodate everyone. Apparently, a group of parents complained because a tall, teenage boy on the bus was victimizing their children. He was sliding his hand under their clothes while they cried for him to stop. They would fight to keep from having to, but the driver would order the children to sit with him so that she could continue her route. Eventually, one child told a parent and other accounts of sexual assault surfaced.

Trey was expelled from school and juvenile charges were filed. Figuratively pausing to analyze the situation, it appears that he never actually left his father despite the 500-mile cushion between them. Trey fought the battle within his head and lost, heeding to the advice of the wrong voices, the echoes of his father's seductive wrath against his own son. The victim becomes the perpetrator. It became easier to understand Trey's sister, still finding it difficult to overcome her own warped, dysfunctional existence. Now it has spread to a new family that must deal with this properly before the memories become parasitic time bombs each has to bear forever.

I know that the teachers do not blame themselves. It is not the fault of the educational leaders or politicians, because they could not possibly have seen this coming. It was a spontaneous, random act of cruel dehumanization. Unforeseeable. How could it have anything to do with the curriculum? How could cooperative assignments and networking have prevented something as horrible as this? Perhaps the fact that Trey scored below proficiency on the end of grade tests the previous May had something to do with his actions. The importance of passing test scores was preached monotonously all year, and then he failed. Maybe this had something to do with his low self-esteem, humility, and despair. Does that mean the schools created a child molester? There is no way of telling if the inferiority of not winning a significant award, or being humiliated with an insignificant one, lead to a lost sense of belonging in the school. How can our government measure the impact of failing scores after the test has been promoted all year as the sole measure of a student's worth? Nobody will ever know.

But if the school had been truly cooperative, if his rivals were actually friends, and if employees recognized the signs of abuse and worked to rebuild him, is it possible these things would not have occurred? If the school built a network around Trey and supported him, would he have withdrawn like he did that summer? If Trey felt positive growth through an effort of the school to build his resiliency, would he have found it necessary to exploit weaker children? If he had passed the end-of-grade tests, then he would not have spent the first two weeks of the summer awaiting the principal's social promotion, feeling inadequate and on the brink of failure yet a third time. Looking at Trey from his perspective is the only way to see how his fate might have been altered. Instead, the school labeled him instead of challenging him, inadvertently creating a situation where he could only lose instead of a climate where he felt wanted. They watched him like prison guards instead of assisting him like mentors. The public will never wonder if the school nurtured this adolescent pedophile when they smugly critique the judge's decision. School staff will probably not use the event to look inward to determine their responsibility in this matter. For these are the times when we distance ourselves from the fallen, when the injured child lies critically wounded and we immediately begin the separation between what we know we can do and what we are willing to do.

Trey sits at home with the ghosts of his father's treachery blackening his gloomy philosophies of happiness and duty. The horror of knowing that you have become that which you feared most in life is one of the most sobering realizations for a human. Shame and sorrow are now compounded upon the feelings of inadequacy and horridly low self-esteem. Guilt contaminates every relationship until it becomes numbness, void of ambition. This is the point at which the child loses all hope, and equally tragic, his innocence forever. I saw him several months later and he was not a child any longer. As if a taxidermist had gutted him, there was no life beyond his eyes like there once was. I felt shame and anger; he felt nothing, and would probably continue to do so.

ME

I sometimes wonder why I quit teaching English and entered the field of educational leadership; I enjoyed introducing high school seniors to Milton and Chaucer, walking through Elsinor with a troubled youth named Hamlet, and exploring the frustrations of young adults found in the poetry of Keats, Shelley, and Byron, the big three Romantics. John Donne's melancholy wisdom and Wordsworth's beautiful and vivid descriptions of Tintern Abbey have moments that would give even the most distant seniors chills, and I loved running those emotions up their backs until they shivered. I had a complete arsenal of memorized quotes that I could apply to nearly every one of their teenage insecurities, often showing them the power and value of literature as a resource. Although my teaching style marched to the beat of its own drum,

I think I was as good as Mr. Michael on some days, and better on one or two others.

Throughout the spring of the year I would intentionally drop philosophical quotes from an unknown source, and occasionally the students would call me on it, asking me who wrote it, or where they could find it. I would respond by suggesting that it was some book written by a famous writer, but his name escapes me. I added that I became familiar with his writing as a child, but thought he was very silly then; as an adult, I have found him to be very profound. But I could conveniently never remember his name, so I would get back to the topic of the day, leaving them curious and determined to make me remember. Some figured it out but I lied and told them they were wrong. I always left them with something to think about, some shred of wisdom we stumbled over in the lesson earlier without giving it much thought, and then retrieving it just before the bell, before they entered the world of crowded halls, stuffed lockers, and the aroma of industrial pizza.

It started as a fun thing to do, but ended as a rite of passage in my high school. I told the students that they may think they have all grown up, but we were going to end school on the last day of classes (before testing and graduation) the way it began thirteen years earlier. Each year the seniors exaggerated the significance of the event more, until some were wearing pajamas and bringing teddy bears and blankets to class. It was a way for them to have fun and make the underclassmen envious of their senior status, so it quickly became an overly pompous activity they all seemed to anticipate.

During that last day, I would wait to read them a story at the end of class, having them crowd around me as I sat in a chair with a picture book that took ten minutes to read, even when I showed everyone the illustrations. I wasn't wearing my "Save-the-Children" power tie or sporting a team of photographers following every movement, but I would give the command and these seniors would crowd around me like the carefully selected children on the cover of Governor Hunt's book. Plopping onto the floor, each mocked the eagerness for adventure by faking childish enthusiasm. It was, of course, a joke, a funny deviation from the norm and a way for them to feel nostalgic, infantile, and grown all at once. It was a celebration of a journey' completion and the beginning of a new one, the completion of a circle. Not to be taken seriously, it was a moment where it was acceptable to laugh at each other and, of course, at me, especially when I pulled from my bag a large, colorful book written by everyone's favorite at one time or another, Dr. Seuss.

But at the end, some would be crying. They would reflectively realize that I had set them up, but they weren't angry; they seemed to know that it was my graduation gift to them in the same manner I taught literature all year long. As I read the text and oscillated the illustrations (For the record, those elementary teachers who can read a book upside down are phenomenal), we would stumble over familiar words and phrases. Not because the students had read the book as children; they had not. *Oh, the Places You'll Go* teaches students about the negative effects of competition and how they will not always be victorious, the darkness that lies behind life's glamour, and the battles they will fight with themselves. It poetically discusses resiliency and how it helps students venturing out into the world, but how some without it will be left behind. The quotes I threw at them in Confucius-style bites of wisdom were from this famous children's author. As I dramatically read the book, knowing when to pause for effect, I studied the faces in the crowd as carefully as they studied the meaningless pictures. I watched the frivolity slowly drain from their eyes and as the giggling was pushed aside by prophetic phrases that splashed them with melancholy, pride, fear, and hope.

As I was known to do, I tricked them. In the midst of their riotous celebration of themselves, I slipped a drop of somber reality into their spirited toasts. I would try to pace the reading so the final words would fall just before the climactic bell in the final English class that they would ever attend in high school; I hoped that they would walk out into the hall for the last time with the same sense of beginning as they did years before. Even though they mocked their child selves in the humorous tradition of bringing robes to English class while pretending to suck on thumbs, I hope they learned that the child within still lives and must, like all children, be respected and nurtured. Even *that* child is not to be left behind, but cradled and heard. You can't tell students this, you can't even show them this; you simply create the environment and provide the stimulus. The rest must happen on its own.

I still lack the satisfaction of knowing that I have survived the trauma of my childhood because its shadows still darken my perspectives at times, constant reminders that I am never immune to its devastating powers. Struggling to understand normalcy, if there is such a thing, I try not to let simple, harmless actions overwhelm me. I am also cognitive of the fact that I often become numb when others around me crumble into emotional seizures. I am different in this respect. My sense of humor is my shield and my lance, used to keep people from getting too close and reminding them that I am no one to take lightly. Yet I love laughter because it is the purist form of freedom, a way to momentarily remove the parasites that cripple minds, and to savor life's ultimate moments.

I am one of the survivors, a successful "feel-good" story that entitles me to have a voice. I suppose one might consider me a winner of sorts, but I resent that because it is based on the assumption that others had to fail for me to get where I am. All can win. The starting lines are different and the finish is undefined, so lets not apply our national gluttony for competition to systemically crown victors in races that blind tradition, industrialism, and political arrogance have created. It is my power, whether earned or not, that I hope to use for those who are abused and think that they will never be heard, unless in the form of a muffled whimper in a darkened room. The issues that threatened me as a boy still haunt me as an adult, thwarting any overconfidence that my childhood's drama is behind me. My position is my gift, simply an opportunity to help those who are physically and mentally unable to seek it themselves. They are shattered children from unstable and broken homes who go to school every day, only to have their inferiority confirmed in a competitive, judgmental, and sometimes hostile environment.

Recently the deaths of my parents and the familial altercations that followed led to a meltdown of sorts, and I was quickly put on medication for depression. Two years later, "bipolar" would be the corrected diagnosis, and my medication was changed. Not, however, before I emotionally hurt my wife, switched jobs, sold my truck (I loved that truck), spent a bunch of money, and told off my boss, a school superintendent who, retrospectively, deserved every word. Apparently the medication caused a disruption to the ebb and flow of emotions, causing me to get "stuck" in mania, the flow without the ebb. My psychologist suggested that it was as if I had been prescribed cocaine. Now the medication I take to stay "normal" seems to be working, but it could be that the demons have gone back into hibernation and I am only experiencing a false sense of security. But a false sense of security is better than a real sense of fear, so I will bask in the illusion of my temporary sun if that is what it is, until the next bit of distant thunder uncontrollably rolls through my head, arousing the ever-present beasts from their slumber.

From an outsider's perspective, this is success for a child who endured abuse and neglect. To the few who know this story, my resiliency is celebrated and glorified, as if the dragon I thought I defeated will never recover, or the Hydra will not sprout another head as soon as I turn my back. They see the glimpses of accomplishments and the triumphs, my defensive joking and jovial sidestepping, the college degrees, and assume that I walk this planet unscathed by my childhood's nightmarish degradation. Like a terminal disease, its effects can be slowed, disguised, or even kept in submission, but it is always inside and must be tended to properly. Perhaps death is the only escape, but the horrors are unbearable when faced alone.

Even though I have made a difference for some, there are too many that I must leave behind in the current educational system. I recognize these kids without knowing anything about them, filing by me in the hallways between classes, hurrying to the restrooms before the bullies arrive, or running to the cafeteria because they fear they may not be fed. I see the lack of sleep in their eyes after a long night and I see those eyes fill with fear when I have to call home to report a disciplinary problem. I have clutched knives in my hand that I confiscated from children who brought them to school to end the daily bullying; I have fatherly embraced hysterical runaways who didn't run far enough. Abusive parents with vein-ridden throats and red faces have pointed fingers in my face because I questioned their child about injuries or the nature of unusual comments. I have seen children find the courage and self-control to speak when my questioning broaches sensitive areas. I see the product of child abuse *every single day.*

I do not feel successful, except for the fact that I have broken the cycle in my family so that my children will never fear me or eventually be feared. I have made the most of what I was given, done the best with what I knew, and listened not to the temptresses that feed on the weak. Special adults guided me, but were never in my life long. In fact, my Aunt Linda (Dad's sister) and her husband Denny, whom we have been close to all of our lives, still do not seem to realize what I went through, but I rarely discuss it. And even though I am a mutt in my middle-aged years, I need to know that there are adults in the world who love and care about me.

There is no conclusion, only a cessation because the points I intended to make have been made. Some segments were very difficult to write because watery eyes choked progress, or anger erupted and ended the word processing for that day. I am not to be the recipient of pity; that privilege should go to the children who come from homes where rules of decency are outweighed by the cyclical inhumanity that manifests itself in what might very well be the highest form of cruelty on earth. The children whose weary heads never land on caring shoulders, or whose tears are never brushed aside by loving hands. I hope this effort finds its way from this tiny stream to the mighty ocean that embodies school reform and is found to be of value. I hope that Phillip, Starla, David, Alex, and Trey will not become faded memories, lives wasted by the adults who found a violent response to personal frustrations through the hostile humiliation and complete degradation of children. I hope there will be something salvaged from their broken childhoods that can help mend their lives and those who follow them.

My life is at best half over, and I resent the abuse, not the abusers. To rise above it all, there must first be peace. My father was a frustrated man unprepared for fatherhood and also the victim of abuse. Mom was a bipolar alcoholic who had less control over her actions than she will ever realize. Their damage has given me insights to help children I might never have seen without it. I am proud that I remained true to my sense of justice and that I kept the childhood promises I made to myself while lying in pain on the bottom bunk so many years ago. I am thankful that my inner child spoke and even more thankful that I listened. Mr. Michael will never know how dramatically he salvaged the life of a bashful student nearly 30 years ago, how he guided me from a painful obscurity to a sometimes overly-brash state of resiliency, how his dead writers became the apothecaries I needed to flourish. I am sure he never realized that his interventions worked so well, that he is the founder of a pyramiding scheme where his acts of kindness are exponentially reaching strangers both living and yet to be born. I wonder how many remember him as fondly, or how many others will never know the source of their salvation. The words he chose for me are not vague now. A crazy teacher's sweaty note changed my life. Mr. Michael is "my giant."

My life has not been graceful; much of the time spent in a tailspin or on a collision course, but there has been flight. It was not a pretty liftoff by any means, bouncing down the runway like the pilot of a plane with a payload beyond its capacity, but I became airborne and flew because there were adults in the control tower who guided me. And now, when my flight hits turbulence and the night reeks of blackness, I still see their beacon atop the distant tower, the one that rises above senseless cruelty and the blindness of habit, and the murky skies open, and a favorable wind somehow finds its way to my wings. And I hope that millions more will follow, empowered with the resiliency to live without fear and to leave behind their torturous lives of quiet desperation.

Bibliography

"Acts of Omission: An Overview of Child Neglect," *National Clearinghouse on Child Abuse and Neglect* <www.childwelfare.gov> Washington, D.C.: U.S. Department of Health and Human Services, 2001.

Adler, Mortimer. *The Paideia Program: An Educational Syllabus*. New York: MacMillan, 1984.

Austin, James. "Alternatives to Competition in Music Education," *Educational Digest* 55 (1990): 45–49.

Ayers, William and Janet Miller eds. *A Light in Dark Times: Maxine Greene and the Unfinished Conversation*. New York: Teacher's College, Columbia UP, 1998.

Barnett, Douglas, Jody Todd Manly, and Dante Cicchetti, "Defining Child Maltreatment: The Interface Between Policy and Research." in *Child Abuse, Child Development and Social Policy,* ed. D. Cicchetti & S. L. Toth. Norwood, NJ: Ablex , 1993.

Bauman, Zygmunt. *Liquid Love.* Cambridge: Polity, 2003.

Becker-Weidman, Arthur. *Child Abuse and Neglect* 2006, <http://www. mental-health-matters.com/articles/article.php?artID=581> (8 March 2006).

Benard, Bonnie. "Fostering Resiliency in Kids," *Educational Leadership* 67, (2001): 44–48.

Bennis, Warren. *On Becoming a Leader.* New York: Basic Books, 2003.

Brophy, Jere. "Supporting Students' Confidence as Learners." *Motivating Students to Learn.* Boston: McGraw-Hill, 1998.

Brown, Rexford. *Schools of Thought.* San Francisco: Jossey-Bass, 1993.

Brubaker, Dale. *Creative Curriculum Leadership.* Thousand Oaks, CA: Corwin, 1994.

Cameron-McCabe, Nelda, Martha M. McCarthy and Stephen B.Thomas. *Public School Law.* Boston: Pearson, 2004.

Camus, Albert. "Quotes on Young People," *The Freechild Project* 1948, <http://www .freechild.org/quotations.htm> (May 20, 2006).

"(The) Case for High School Activities," *National Federation of State High School Associates* 2003, <http://www.nfhs.org/web/2004/01/the_case_for_highschool _activities.aspx> (28 March 2006).

"Child Abuse and Neglect: The Emotional Effects." *The Royal College of Psychiatrists* 2005, <http://www.rcpsych.ac.uk.info/mhgu/newmhgu19.htm> (1 March 2005).

"Child Abuse Statistics." *Children's Defense Fund.* 2002. <http://www.childdefense.org> (11 Dec. 2003).

Cohen, Judith. "Practice Parameters for the Assessment and Treatment of Children and Adolescents with Posttraumatic Stress Disorder." *American Academy of Child Adolescent Psychiatry* 37, no. 9 (October, 1998): 997–1001.

Coles, Robert. *Their Eyes Meeting the World: The Drawings and Paintings of Children.* New York: Houghton Mifflin, 1992.

Darling-Hammond, Linda. *The Right to Learn: A Blueprint for Creating Schools that Work.* San Francisco: Jossey-Bass, 1997.

"Data and Statistics." *Action for Children: North Carolina.* 2002, <http://www.ncchild.org/content/view/274/158/> (2 February 2003).

Dennis, Wayne. *Children of the Creche.* New York: Appleton-Century Crofts, 1973.

Edmonds, Ron. "School Violence Prevention: Protective Processes Within Schools." *U.S. Department of Health and Human Services.* <http://www. mentalhealth.org/schoolviolence/part1chp14.asp> (27 Dec. 2005).

Friere, Paulo. *Pedagogy of the Oppressed.* New York: Continuum, 2003.

Greene, Maxine. *The Dialectic of Freedom.* New York: Teacher's College Press, 1988.

Hamblen, Jessica. "PTSD in Children and Adolescents." *National Center for Post Traumatic Stress Disorder, U.S. Department of Veteran Affairs* 2007, <http://www.ncptsd.va.gov/ncmain/ncdocs/fact_shts/fs_children.html> (3 June 2007).

Hanson, Carol. "High anxiety," *Teacher Magazine* 10, no. 5 (1999): 36.

Hellstedt, Jon, "Kids, Parents and Sport: Some Questions and Answers. *The Physician and Sportsmedicine* 16, no. 4, (April, 1988): 59–71.

"Helping Abused Children," *Neshaminy (Pa) School District* 2003, <http: //www.neshaminy.k12.pa.us> (10 Aug. 2005).

Howard, Sue and Bruce Johnson, "What makes the difference? Children and Teachers Talk about Resilient Outcomes for Children 'At-risk'," *Educational Studies*, 26, no. 3 (2000): 135.

Hunt, Jim. *First in America: An Educational Governor Challenges North Carolina.* Raleigh, NC: First in America Foundation, 2001.

Hyman, Irwin. "The Enemy Within: Tales of Punishment, Politics, and Prevention." Paper presented at the Annual National Convention of School Psychologists, Atlanta, GA., March 1996.

"Inmate histories: Evidence of child abuse." *Alaska Justice Forum*, 15, no. 3, 1998, <http://justice.uaa.alaska.edu/forum/f153fa98/a_inmante.html> (8 March 2005).

Jew, C.L., K.E. Green, & June Kroger, "Development and Validation of a Measure of Resiliency." *Measurement and Evaluation in Counseling & Development* 32, no. 2 (1999): 79.

Kozol, Jonathan. *Ordinary Resurrections.* New York: Perennial, 2000.

Kritsberg, Wayne. *The Adult Children of Alcoholics Syndrome.* (New York: Bantam, 1985): 56.

Kohn, Alfie. *No Contest: The Case Against Competition* Boston: Houghton Mifflin, 1986.

——. *The Schools our Children Deserve: Moving Beyond Traditional Classrooms and "Tougher Standards."* Boston: Houghton Mifflin, 1999.

Krovetz, Marty. "Fostering Resiliency," *Thrust for Educational Leadership*, 28, no. 5, (1999): 28.

——. "Resiliency: A Key Element for Supporting Youth At-risk," *The Clearing House* 73, no. 2, (1999): 121–124.

Lion King, The. Walt Disney Pictures, (1994).

Lock, R.H. and M. Janas. "Build Resiliency." *Intervention in School & Clinic* 38, no. 2 (2002): 117.

Lowenthal, Barbara. "The Effects of Maltreatment and Ways to Promote Children's Resiliency." *Childhood Education* 75, no. 4 (1999): 204–09.

Lynn, Andrea. *Primate Research Says Competition not Driving Force* 2002, <http://unisci.com/stories/20021/0218021.htm> (8 January 2005).

McGregor, Douglas. *The Human Side of Enterprise*. New York: McGraw-Hill, 1985.

Melhuish, Ted. "Child Protective Services," *Wikipedia*, 2007. <http://en. wikipedia .org/wiki/Child_protective_services#In_the_public_eye> (3 June 2007).

Miller, G., and J.Greenwood. "Letter in Support of Child Welfare Funding." *National Association of Social Workers.* 2004, <http://www.naswc.org> (22 Sept. 2005).

Money, John. "Child Abuse: Growth Failure, IQ Deficit, and Learning," *Journal of Learning Disabilities* 15, no. 10 (1982).

Mrazek, David and Patricia. Mrazrek. "Resilience in Child Maltreatment Victims: A Conceptual Exploration." *Child Abuse and Neglect*, 11 (1987): 357–365.

"Myths about Posttraumatic Stress Disorder." *PTSD Alliance* 2006, <http://www .ptsdalliance.org> (5 March 2006).

"National Child Abuse Statistics." *Childhelp USA*. 2005, <http://www.childhelp usa.org> (5 March 2006).

Neuberger, Julia. "Brain Development Research: Wonderful Window of Opportunity to Build Public Support for Childhood Education," *Young Children* 52, no.1 (1997): 4–9.

Ney, Phillip, Tak Fung, and Adele Wickett, "The Worst Combinations of Child Abuse and Neglect," *Child Abuse and Neglect,* 18, no.9, (1994): 705–714.

O'Brien, Shirley. "A Heavy Price for Heroics." *The Association for Childhood International,* <http://www.udel.edu/bateman/acei/childabuse.pdf> (1991): 4.

Padron, Yolanda, Hesholt Waxman, and Shwu-Yong Huang. "Classroom Behaviors and Learning Environment Differences Between Resilient and Nonresilient Elementary School Students." *Journal of Education for Students Placed at Risk* 4, no. 1, (1999): 65–82.

Perry, Bruce, David Conrad, Christine Dobson, Stephanie Schick, and Duane Runyan, "The Children's Crisis Care Center Model." *Child Trauma Academy, Department of Psychiatry and Behavioral Medicine, Baylor College of Medicine*. 2004, <www.ChildTrauma.org> (1 March 2006).

Perry, Bruce. "Neurodevelopment and the Neurophysiology of Trauma I: Conceptual Considerations for Clinical Work with Maltreated Children. *APSAC Advisor* 6, no. 1, (1993): 1–18.

——. "How Children Become Resilient." *Scholastic Parent and Child* 10, no. 2 (2002): 33.

——. "Neurobiological Sequelae of Childhood Trauma: Post-traumatic Stress in Children." *Catecholamines in Post-traumatic Stress Disorder Emerging Concepts* (Washington, D.C.: American Psychiatric Press, 2004): 253–276.

——. "Traumatized Children: How Childhood Trauma Influences Brain Development." *Baylor College of Medicine* 2000. <http://www.bcm.tmc.edu/cta/trau CAMI .htm> (22 Feb. 2005).

Public School Laws of North Carolina. Charlottesville, VA: LexisNexis, 2001.

Purpel, David. *The Moral and Spiritual Crisis in Education: A Curriculum for Social Justice and Compassion,* (New York: Bergin and Garvey, 1989).

——. *Moral Outrage in Education*. New York: Peter Lang, 2001.

Reyome, Nancy. "A Comparison of the School Performance of Sexually Abused, Neglected, and Non-maltreated Children." *Child Study Journal* 23, no. 1 (1993): 17–39.

Richardson, Glenn. "High School Curriculum Fosters Resiliency." *Education Digest,* 63, no. 6 (1998): 23.

Romeo, Felecia. "Child Abuse and Report Cards," *Education* 120, no. 3 (Spring 2000): 438.

Sechrist, William. "Why Teach About Child Abuse and Neglect?" *Education Digest,* 66, no. 2 (2000): 45.

Sedlak, Andrea and Diana Broadhurst. "Executive Summary of the Third National Incidence Study of Child Abuse and Neglect." *U.S. Department of Health and Human Services: Administration for Children and Families.* 1996, http://www.acf.org (5 March 2006).

Senge, Peter. *Schools that Learn* New York: Doubleday, 2000.

Shore, Rima. *Rethinking the Brain.* (New York: Families and Work Institute, 1997): 40.

Skinner, B. F. *The Shaping of a Behaviorist.* New York: Knopf, 1979.

"State Child Welfare Agency Survey." *National Data Analysis System*, 2001, <http://www.ndas.cwla.org/Report.asp?PageMode=&Report> (11 May 2004).

Steinem, Gloria. *Revolution From Within,* (Boston: Little, Brown, 1992): 75.

Sullivan, Robert. "What Makes a Child Resilient?" *Time* 157, no.11 (2001), 35–38.

Tyack, David. *The One Best System: A History of American Urban Education.* Cambridge: Harvard UP, 1974.

"What is Child Abuse and Neglect?" *National Foundation for Abused and Neglected Children* 1997, <http://www.gangfreekids.org> (15 March, 2004).

"What Parents Should Know," *Prevent Child Abuse America*, <www.preventchildabuse .org/publications/parents/downloads/recognizing_abuse.pdf> (2003).

Wisconsin Department of Public Instruction, 1997. <http://www.dpi.wi. giov./sped/pdf/athletics.pdf> (26 March 2006).